Hobbyist Guide
—— To ——
Catfish And Loaches

Hobbyist Guide
—— To ——
Catfish And Loaches

Dr. Paul V. Loiselle
Dr. David Pool

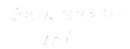

© 1993
Tetra-Press
Tetra-Werke Dr. rer nat. Ulrich Baensch GmbH
P.O. Box 1580. D-49304 Melle, Germany
All right reserved, incl. film, broadcasting,
television as well as the reprinting
1st edition 1-10.000, 1993
Printed in Germany by Busse Druck
DLB-30.313-93

Distributed in the U.S.A. by
Tetra Sales U.S.A.,
3001 Commerce Street
Blacksburg, VA 24060

Distributed in UK by
Tetra Sales
Lambert Court, Chestnut Avenue
Eastleigh, Hampshire S05 3ZQ
WL-Code: 16580

ISBN 3-89356-138-2

Contents

EDITORIAL COMMENTS

One of the remarkable as-pects of the sociology of ornamental fish keeping is the way in which an initial experience with a single species can influence future perception of its entire family. The rowdy behavior of the chanchito, *Heros facetus,* the first cichlid imported into Germany, led to the entire Family Cichlidae being branded as the terrorists of the aquarium world, a reputation it has yet to live down! In a perverse fashion, the positive image enjoyed by the catfishes of the genus *Corydoras* has had an equally undesirable impact on the popular perception of catfish as aquarium residents. It is a safe bet that nine out of every ten aquarists, recalling the droll little scavengers of their first aquarium, automatically assume that all catfish are innocuous bewhiskered bottom-dwellers that manage quite nicely on the leftovers of the tank's "real" inhabitants.

This tendency to regard catfish as nothing more than animated tank accessories, an attitude that also embraces the taxonomically distant but ecologically analogous loaches, leads to a policy of unintentional neglect that has condemned thousands of these fish to brief lives of semi-starvation. Furthermore, this attempt to impose a most restrictive

Synodontis decorus Photo: P. V. Loiselle

stereotype upon such a marvelously diverse group as the Suborder Siluroidei often has immediate and negative repercussions upon the other fishes with which catfish are housed. The conventional wisdom notwithstanding, the great majority of caffish are not harmless scavengers but rather chillingly efficient predators capable of overcoming prey a respectable proportion of their own length. As more than one retailer will attest the unsuspected depredations of such species as the Asian bumblebee cat, *Leiocassis siamensis,* or *Pimelodella pictus* are frequently responsible for a brisk repeat business in neon tetras or harlequin rasboras!

Happily, there is a growing tendency to regard catfish - and their distant relatives the loaches - as highly desirable aquarium residents in their own right. Certain representatives of each group, like *Botia macrantha,* the clown loach, *Liasomadoras oncinus,* the jaguar catfish, or *Synodontis angelicus,* occupy, by virtue of their striking coloration and relative rarity, a secure place among the select company of "status fish" Others, like the kuhli loaches of the genus *Acanthopthalmus* or the bristle-nose catfish of the genus *Ancistrus* are appreciated for their unusual - some might even say bizarre - appearance. Species such as the weatherfishes of the genus *Misgumus* and the electric catfish, *Malapterurus electricus* command interest by virtue of their distinctive behavior. Finally, a substantial number of catfishes and loaches are simply appreciated for their aesthetic contribution to an aquarium. A community tank without its complement of *Corydoras* is certainly much less interesting than one that sports a school of these active bottom dwellers.

With increased interest in catfish and loaches has come an increased demand for information on their husbandry. While there is general agreement that there is more to keeping these fish in good condition than dropping them into an aquarium and forgetting about them, the aquarium literature is often less than complete in its coverage of both their maintenance requirements and their characteristics as aquarium residents. This is hardly surprising. Catfish alone comprise thirty distinct families, some, like the Bagridae or the Loricariidae, containing hundreds of species. The sheer scope of the subject precludes any pretense of comprehensive coverage. Of equal importance, the current upsurge of interest in caffish and loaches is a relatively recent phenomenon. While it has proven most productive of useful information on the care and breeding of these fishes, insufficient time has passed for this body of facts to work its way into the aquaristic mainstream.

My object in this Collectors Edition is to bring together a useful collection of essays that concentrate on the husbandry of catfish and loaches. The limitations of this format obviously preclude a complete coverage of this large and diverse assemblage of fishes. I have thus been necessarily selective in my choice of subjects. On the one hand, this monograph devotes considerable space to groups of long-standing availability, for which a considerable corpus of information is available. On the other, it makes an effort to gather together data on representatives of groups whose commercial availability is of much more recent date. Whenever possible, I have included information on the reproductive patterns of these fishes. Aquarists within the last decade have made the discovery that when properly nourished and given a modicum of attention, many catfish species spawn quite freely in captivity.

There is every reason to hope that many more species will respond to similar treatment. Given the size of the group, surprisingly little is known about catfish reproductive biology. The serious caffish enthusiast is thus well placed to make important contributions to the existing body of information on the natural history of these fascinating fishes. The growing interest in both catfishes and loaches is reflected in the existance of several national speciality clubs devoted to disseminating information on the biology and husbandry of these fishes. A list of these groups, together with the addresses of appropriate contact persons may be found on the last page of this issue. I strongly urge readers with a serious interest in these fishes to join one or more of these groups. Quite apart from the useful information contained in their publications, these organizations afford a major opportunity for like-minded aquarists to enjoy the sort of fellowship that makes tropical fish keeping such a rewarding hobby.

Dr. Paul V. Loiselle
Co-Ordinating Editor

Page 10/11: Synodontis decorus ▶
Photo: B. Kahl

A fishing man in a brazilian catfish-biotop.

ALL ABOUT LOACHES

The true loaches of the Family Cobitiidae are representatives of the huge suborder Cyprinoidei. They are thus fairly close relatives of the true minnows of the Family Cyprinidae, notwithstanding their superficial resemblance to several catfish families, themselves members of the more distantly related suborder Siluroidei. The loaches are a predominantly Eurasian group. Though a few European species occur in the Mediterranean-draining rivers of north Africa, only a single representative of the genus *Noemacheilus,* endemic to the Ethiopian highlands, has ever been taken from sub-Saharan Africa. Loaches are quintessential bottom dwellers, many species burrowing into the substratum when pursued by enemies. Slender-bodied species such as the kuhli loaches of the genus *Acanthopthalmus* are particularly adept at such evasive manuvers. The deeper-bodied loaches of the genera *Botia* and *Noemacheilus* while more inclined to swim about in midwater, also defend individual territories centered on a refuge of some sort. Failure to provide a sufficiency of such shelters can result in damaging fights between loaches and other,

The European weatherfish, Misgurnus fossilis, is an attractive cold-water loach.

Noemacheilus barbatulus, the European loach.

comparably motivated tank residents. Many species have a marked preference for swiftly-flowing water in nature. These will prosper only if some effort is made to provide comparable conditions in captivity.

Loach anatomy reflects their bottom-dwelling existance. Their mouths open downwards and are surrounded by numerous fleshy barbels well equipped with sensitive taste receptors. Their eyes are small and frequently covered over with a transparent fold of skin. Loach scales, when present at all, tend to be small and deeply imbedded in the skin. Their swim bladder is often strongly reduced and seldom fullyfunctional, hardly a disadvantage to bottom livers confronted with the task of holding position in the face of a strong current. Interestingly, many species can make use of atmospheric oxygen. They swallow a gulp of air and utilize the intestine as an auxillary respiratory organ, rather in the manner of many South American armored catfish families. The vertical fins are small, but the paired fins, particularly the pectorals, are powerfully developed. The fins are devoid of spines, but all genera possess a switch-balde-like bony spine below each eye. When erected, these are formidable weapons.

Loaches are easily maintained aquarium residents. They do best in planted tanks with clean, fine-grained gravel bottoms. As noted, they require access to suitable shel-

A tropical representative of the genus, Noemacheilus (Acanthocobitis) botia, native to India.

ter to prosper They do not appreciate very hard, alkaline water, but seem otherwise indifferent about its chemical makeup. Most species are sensitive to elevated nitrite levels. Regular partial water changes and reliance on biological filtration provide loaches with a healthy aquarium environment. The Tetra Brillant sponge filter constitutes an efficient and unobtrusive means to this end. Loaches are easily fed bottom feeders. They accept any of the usually available live, frozen and prepared foods. All species do extremely well on a staple diet of TabiMin and TetraTips. These foods are particularly useful because they sink immediately to the bottom and are thus less likely to be pirated by a tank's surface and midwater feeding residents. Feeding the loaches after the tank's other residents are satiated provides additional assurance that the loaches will get their share of food.

Six loach genera are regularly kept as aquarium residents. The weatherfishes of the genera *Cobitis* and *Misgurnus* are Eurasian coldwater loaches. They derive their common name from their extreme sensitivity to changes in barometric pressure. This causes them to swim about in an agitated manner with the onset of a low pressure front, behavior that makes them fairly accurate predictors of a storm's approach. These loaches do not appreciate temperatures in excess of 24° C. (c. 75° F.). Hence they are not good candidates for a tropical display tank. However, they prosper in a cold water aquarium and take well

The recently imported Ceylon loach, Noemacheilus cf. notostigma.

Photo: P. V. Loiselle

enough to outdoor pond living to breed regularly therein. Though individuals can reach lengths of 20.0 cm (c. 8"), these are innocuous loaches that make good community tank residents. Weatherfishes scatter their numerous greenish eggs among the roots and leaves of aquatic plants, providing them with no care once spawning is completed.

The genus *Noemacheilus* comprises both temperate zone and tropical species. Representatives of the latter are episodically available and should be handled in the same manner as the smaller *Botia* species. The horsefaced loach, *Acanthopsis choirorhynchus,* is a southeast Asian species adept at „swimming" through the aquarium gravel. It is a peaceful species capable of reaching, 15.0 cm (c. 6") standard length. When housed with small, schooling species, it will spend most of the

daylight hours foraging in the open. Kept with larger, more aggressive tankmates such as cichlids, the horse-faced loach will stay buried much of the time and emerge to forage once the lights go off. There are no reports of captive spawnings of either of these two loach genera.

Most of the loaches available to aquarists are representatives of the large Asian genus *Botia.* These are short-bodied, laterally compressed fishes with strongly developed territorial instincts. The genus spans great diversity in size. The dwarf loach, *B. sidthimnuki,* barely reaches 5.0 cm (c. 2") overall length, while *B. macrantha,* the colorful clown loach, can grow up to 40.0 cm (c. 16") long. These tropical loaches thrive over a temperature range of 24°-30° C. (c. 75°-85° F.). All *Botia* species are markedly territorial, and most will defend a shelter ferociously against both conspe-

Above: The horse-faced loach, Acanthopsis choirorhynchus.

*Right: The popular khulii loach, Acanthophthalmus kuhlii.
Photo: B. Kahl*

cific and heterospecific rivals. The clown, dwarf and skunk *(B. horae)* loaches will live together in groups as long as their tank has plenty of hiding places. Peaceful coexistance of individuals of the other species available to hobbyists is a function of tank and group size. Even such highly aggressive species as *B. modesta,* the red-finned loach, can be kept succesfully in groups of four or more, but never as pairs, while the larger the tank, the less the liklihood of serious intramural fighting. Aggressive encounters between two *Botia* are accompanied by strange „clicking" noises. *Botia* species should not be kept with long-finned tankmates such as

angelfish, for some individuals will use their subocular spines to shred the fins of their companions.

There are few reported *Botia* spawnings under aquarium conditions, and no descriptions of their reproductive behavior. These rare events appear to have happened by accident rather than design. Fry have been found only in tanks containing adult loaches exclusively. This suggests that loaches may spawn unnoticed by their keeper in community settings, where egg predation would swiftly obliterate evidence of reproductive activity. Aquarists wishing to breed one of these loaches in captivity would do best to focus their efforts on the smaller representatives of the genus, such as the dwarf and skunk loaches.

The worm or khuli loaches of the genus *Acanthopthalmus* are perennial aquarium favorites, as much for their bizarre snake-like body form as their boldly barred color patterns. These are retiring loaches, quite likely to disappear in a community containing a paucity of plant cover and an abundance of larger, more assertive tankmates. Kuhli loaches are harmless community tank residents and excellent scavengers. They prefer to live in groups and are sometimes found intertwined together in veritable "wormballs" Groups will have periods of almost frenetic activity thought by some to be connected with reproduction. Kuhli loaches have been induced to spawn in captivity both with and without the use of pituitary gonadotropic hormones to stimulate oviposition. They are egg-scatterers, whose spawning behavior is reminiscent of that of *Danio aequipinnatus* and the larger *Barbus* species. The resulting young should be treated in the same manner as barb or danio fry. If care is taken to avoid fouling their tank, they are easily reared. Loaches are desirable aquarium residents, as much for their efficient policing of the tank bottom for uneaten food as for their unusual body forms and often atractive coloration. As long as due consideration is given to their requirements for living space and shelter, they are a worthwhile addition to any community of ornamental fishes. *Dr. P.V.Loiselle*

The dwarf loach, Botia sidthimunki, is the smallest known Botia species.

THE CLEANING HABITS OF ACANTHOPHTHALMUS

I should just like to report on an unusual observation I have made, namely how kuhli loaches have been acting as "cleanerfish" for discus. In my 300 litre tank I keep four very attractive half-grown blue discus and four kuhli loaches *(Acanthophtthalmus semicintus)*. One evening I was quite startled to find that one discus was resting with its head pointing diagonally downwards towards the tank bottom. It was almost black in colour. Whenever a discus takes on this kind of colouration, it is usually a bad sign, at least as far as I can tell from my experience. It is either ill or displaying some kind of adverse reaction to a deterioration in water conditions.

The other three discus fish were not showing any signs of this discolouration. As I already mentioned, the one discus was remaining motionless in one spot, with its head down. It was at this point that I noticed one of the worm-like kuhli loaches swimming around this fish, working its way along the lenght of the discus and upwards and downwards. It seemed to be feeling out the discus' body with its belly, as if it was looking for something. The discus was in no way put out by this activity on the part of the kuhli loaches. It did not find the attention unpleasant or it would have swum away!

This game went on for more than a quarter of an hour, after which the discus started swimming around the tank again, resplendent in its full colouring.

The same thing happened the next evening with one of the other discus, with this fish behaving in exactly the same way as the other. I was not able to establish whether it was the same kuhli loach or not. This cleaning did not turn into a regular event, though I have seen the performance on a number of occasions since then.

To date I have not heard of any instances of freshwater fish behaving in such a way.

The fact that this occurs amongst marine fish is well known, for instance the cleaner wrasse, *Labroides dimidiatus,* which cleans other tank inhabitants by picking any external parasites and damaged tissue off the skin. In my case, this behaviour is worthy of particular attention as the discus and the kuhli loach come from very different habitats and even different countries.

Acanthophthalmus is normally a peaceful, social scavenger and its apparent "cleaning" ability rather surprised me.

Maybe other readers will have noted such behaviour between these two species of fish.

Lothar Schmitz

HAVING FUN WITH LOACHES

Before purchasing loaches (e.g. *Botia* spp.) it is important to familiarise oneself with their natural and prefered aquarium conditions from various books and journals. To a greater or lesser excellent all *Botia* are bottom dwellers, and can adapt to life in the home aquarium quite happily, if a little thought is given to their requirements. I have successfully set up a tank exclusively for keeping loaches.

I obtained rocks with outgrowths of stalactites and stalagmites from local streams with a high chalk con-

tent. I then hollowed out these stones from behind, leaving the more attractive front on display. This was then surrounded by rocks, so that the fish could swim freely in and out. To provide a medium for plant growth, and also to seat the above stones safely on the aquarium floor, well washed sand was added to the tank, and banked up towards the back of the aquarium. The fish may rearrange these stones themselves as they enjoy grubbing around amongst sand and gravel. The stones were arranged along the

(Top to bottom) Barred loach Botia lucasbahi, tiger loach.

(Top to bottom) Botia hymenophysa, red-finned loach, Botia pulchripinnis, Beaufort's loach.

back of the tank and a piece of tree root added for special effects. Some small plants (eg. *Cryptocoryne beckettii)* were planted in the foreground of the aquarium. All species of Botia can be rather erratic swimmers, moving jerkily yet very quickly. To prevent the plants being disturbed too much I added a layer of fine gravel and then a layer of coarse gravel on top of the sand (to a total depth of about 2¼ inches, 6 cm).

With good aeration and filtration, the fish do well at a temperature of 79° F (26° C). New specimens are initially very shy, and often disap-

pear amongst the rocks for several days. If required, a loach tank can be incorporated into a wall with pleasing effects. Because these fish are bottom dwellers, the tank need not be very deep.

I believe that the extent to which different Botia will mix peaceably in the aquarium, depends upon the way in which they are fed. My fish are given plenty of live food *(Tubifex,* Bloodworms, *Daphnia),* much of which I catch myself. Whilst they love live food they will also take flaked food.

Almost all of the species can give off a clicking or crackling sound

21

Botia beauforti, zebra loach.

when at play or when defending their caves. It is usually more noticeable in larger fish (about 6", 15 cm). At the present time there are nine species of *Botia* in my loach tank, plus *Acanthopsis.*

I never have less than three individuals of the same species, and in the case of the dwarf loach *(Botia sidthimunki)* I have nine specimens which all swim around in a small shoal.

My own observations have shown that *Botia* are not completely noc-turnal, as they may all be active to some extent during the day. However, they do like to lie within the protection of plant clusters, on leaves (especially *Botia sidthimunki* and *B. ichachata),* on stones or even just remain within their caves for long periods.

Very little is known about the habits of these lively and interesting fish, and I hope that I have encouraged some aquarists to try their hand at loach keeping.

J. V. Diggelon

◀ *Page 22/23: Botia sidthimunki Photo: B. Kahl*

THE CLOWN LOACH SPAWNED!

Fishes of the *Cobitidae* family are familiar to all aquarists. They are slender, fast moving fish which live on the bottom of the tank and prefer to hide in any cave-like structures provided them. The clown loach is possibly the most popular member of this family, but it requires rather special care. For some reason, this fish is very susceptible to disease in the aquarium - particularly Ichthyophthirius. High temperatures, 27-30° C (80-86° F) are recommended, and the water should be slightly alkaline to reproduce natural conditions. Although these fish are scavengers and grub through the aquarium

The unquestioned aristocrat of the family Cobitidae, the clown loach, Botia macranthus.

gravel in search of food, they should receive their own supply of food and not be expected to live on the excess food left by other fishes. Loaches have rarely spawned in aquaria, probably because the proper natural conditions cannot be created. The following account is an interesting personal experience which shows how unpredictable aquarium fish can be.

A few months ago I received six clown loaches, *Botia macracanthus,* from a friend of mine. They had been maintained in a 320 liter (80 gallon) aquarium for almost five years. The fish were very shy and were seen only once or twice a year when the tank was cleaned. Finally, my friend lost his patience with the fish and sent them to me.

When I received the fish they were six to seven inches in total length. Two of them were very heavy-bodied while the other four were thinner but longer. I decided to house the fish in a 140 liter (35 gallon) tank where a pair of discus had spawned only a few weeks earlier. The tank was planted with 3 large *Echinodorus* from Brazil and there were many pieces of driftwood. The chemical make-up of the water was as follows: pH=6.2, DH=2.0, and nitrite level less than 0.05.

The water temperature was maintained between 29-30 degrees C (84-86 degrees F). An outside power filter was used and the filter medium consisted of a commercial brand of aquarium peat and polyes-

ter filter fibre. As soon as the loaches were placed in their tank, they disappeared into the plants and driftwood. The average observer would have thought the tank was uninhabited. Each evening I would prepare a mixture of Tetramin staple food, shredded beef heart, spinach, and shrimp pellets. This was placed in the front of the tank before the lights were turned off for the night. The food was always gone by the following morning, but no fish were ever observed feeding. In time, the tank gained the title of the "Ghost Tank." On one occasion, I turned out all lights but a dim room light. In a few minutes, the loaches came out of hiding. They moved through the tank in groups of three searching for food. As soon as the main lights were switched on - the fish were gone. They had vanished in an instant!

One day I needed an unusually large plant so I decided to remove one from the "Ghost Tank." As I began to uproot the plant, a cloud of mulm rose into the water. It began to settle after a few seconds, and I was amazed to see 10 to 15 small fish scatter wildly about the tank. I dropped the plant immediately and began to search for the small fish. A close examination revealed very young clown loaches hiding deep in the crown and exposed roots of the two undisturbed plants. After seven weeks, I have found 39 young fish averaging ¾ of an inch in total length. *Werner Nowak*

26

UNUSUAL LOACHES FROM ASIA -
HOMALOPTERIDAE AND GASTEROMYZONTIDAE

The suborder Cyprinoidei includes several families of fishes adapted to life in mountain torrents. Aquarists are most familiar with the so-called Chinese algae eater, *Gyrinocheilus aymonieri*, a representative of the Family Gyrinocheilidae. However, representatives of two other such south Asian rheophile families are

The pectoral and ventral fins overlap in both Gasteromyzon and Pseudogasteromyzon

also imported from time to time, to be sold under such trade names as "Hong Kong plecostomus" or "Chinese suckerbelly loaches" Representatives of the Family Homalopteridae, usually known as hillstream loaches, are characterized by a distinct gap between the pectoral and ventral fins when viewed from above and the presence of small but distinct barbels around the sucker-like mouth. The suckerbelly loaches of the Family Gastromyzontidae lack the oral barbels and when viewed from

above, the pectoral and ventral fins appear to touch or overlap slightly. Modifications of the paired fins and ventral surface allow representatives of both families to adhere tightly to the rocky bottoms of their swifly flowing habitats. As the accompanying illustration clearly shows, a suckerbelly loach can even cling to the glass wall of an aquarium.

The taxonomy of these two families is still very much a matter for specialists. However, the two most commonly exported representatives

Upper: Pseudogasteromyzon cheri
Lower: Homaloptera orthogoniata
3 photos: G. Ott

The rheophilous buffalo catfish, Glyptothorax trilineata shares both its habitat and color pattem with the harlequin hillstream ioach. Photo:P. V. Loiselle

of each have been identified. The harlequin hillstream loach, *Homaloptera orthogoniata,* is native to the island of Borneo and the Malay peninsula. The more plainly marked marbled hillstream loach, *H. zollingeri,* hails from Thailand. The two gastromyzids to date imported are the so-called Hong Kong pleostomus, *Pseudogastromyzon myersi,* and Borneo plecostomus, *Gastromyzon punctulatus.* The last is a lovely little fish, its jet black body covered with many small white spots. Whether representatives of other genera, such as *Balitora, Vanmenia* or *Hemimyzon* have been imported but gone unnoticed is impossible to determine given the prevalent state of knowledge of these fishes among importers and aquarists alike.

It was formerly doubted that these highly specialized fishes could be kept successfully in captivity. It is true that both hillstream and suckerbelly loaches require elevated concentrations of dissolved oxygen

to survive. Their jaw structure is also quite delicate and easily damaged unless great care is taken when moving specimens that have elected to cling to a solid surface. However, if due care is taken when handling these fishes, modern aquarium technology has eliminated the physiological obstacles to their husbandry.

First of all, these fish require strong water movement and ample aeration. Either an inside power filter or a small submersible pump can easily provide the former, while a durable, high performance pump such as the Tetra Luftpump and several airstones are all that is needed to satisfy the latter requirement. Secondly, these fish must be kept relatively cool. The temperature in their tank should not be allowed to exceed 24° C. (c. 75° F.). In warmer water, the metabolic rate of these fishes increases to stressful levels. This increases their demand for oxygen, while simultaneously

Homaloptera zollingeri from Thailand. Photo: G. Ott

reducing the capacity of the aquarium water to retain it in solution. Finally, these fish are extremely intolerant of dissolved metabolic wastes. A program of frequent partial water changes is thus an important adjunct to their succesful maintenance. The mouth shape of both homalopterids and gastromyzontids might lead one to conclude that they feed exclusively upon algae in nature. This is not the case. While these fish do have strong herbivorous tendencies, they also consume a considerable quantity of animal food in nature. The Indian ichthyologist Sunder Lal Hora found that their gut contents included organisms associated with algal mats, such as worms, small freshwater crabs and prawns and aquatic insects and their larvae. In captivity, these fish will eat prepared foods such as Tetra Conditioning Food and Tabi-Min readily. These staples should be supplemented by live or frozen foods such as bloodworms or adult *Artemia* and fresh vegetable foods such as thinly sliced bianched zucchini or leaf lettuce. It is also wise to allow algal growths to develop naturally on the sides and rear of the aquarium. Both hillstream and suckerbelly loaches seem to benefit from the opportunity to "graze" such aquatic meadows. Hopefully, additional representatives of these two interesting families will be imported in the future. Most species grow to no more than 10.0 cm (c. 4") in length, which makes them suitable residents for the home aquarium. As sub-tenants (literally!) of larger community tanks, they are attractively marked subjects whose behavior provides their keeper with much pleasure. Finally, little is known of the natural history of either hillstream or suckerbelly loaches, while their reproductive biology is totally unexplored territory. The serious aquarist can thus make valuable contributions to existing knowledge of these fascinating fishes. *G. Ott*

SPOTLIGHT ON SYNODONTIS

In the catfish family Mochokidae, the genus *Synodontis* is one of the more interesting groups. They are found in freshwater lakes and rivers throughout Africa. Fish of this genus are generally hardy and peaceful, and their bizarre coloration and shape make them fascinating to watch. Physical characteristics include long, feathered barbels, mouths which are large and ventrally directed, large eyes, large heads which are armored on top from the snout to the dorsal fin, and leathery skin. Their large adipose fin is a very unusual adaption.

Most of the species in this genus are muddy green, gray, or brown in color, but a few are quite attractive. Total lengths vary from 6 to 20 cm. (2¼" to 8") in aquaria to as much as 45 cm. (17¾") in the wild for some

(Top to bottom) The true upsidedown catfish, Synodontis nigriventris. Synodontis angelicus.

(Top to bottom) Synodontis flavitaeniatus, Synodontis schoutedeni.

species. The upside-down catfish, *Synodontis nigriventris,* is undoubtedly the most popular *Synodontis* species. Fairly common in its native central Africa, this fish gets its name from the strange habit of swimming belly-up in the water. The coloration of *S. nigriventris* corresponds to its unusual swimming behavior. While most catfish have a lighter ventral than dorsal surface, in this fish the coloration is reversed. Although other *Synodontis* catfish can also swim upside

down, they usually do so only in the shelter of their hiding places. These fish spend much of the day hiding in caves, under over-hanging rocks, among tree roots, or between clumps of plant life. They are nocturnal fish and avoid bright light. In addition to their unusual swimming behavior, *Synodontis* catfish have another strange ability - they squeak. When excited, they make an audible squeaking sound. It seems to be produced by the movement of the dorsal and pecto-

(Top to bottom) Synodontis alberti, Synodontis notatus.

ral fins in their sockets. In aquaria, *Synodontis* rarely have occasion to squeak, although noisy fighting over food or hiding places may occur from time to time. In aggressive situations, the sharply serrated dorsal and pectoral fins of these caffish lock into place for protection.

Synodontis species are easy to maintain in aquaria. The ideal temperature range for these fish is 23-26 degrees (73-79 degrees F), and they are very tolerant in regard to water conditions. Lighting in the tank should not be too bright. The larger *Synodontis* species require big tanks with plenty of hiding places or they will fight incessantly for any dark corner. Usually these caffish are active only at night, but in densely planted aquaria they will leave their hiding places during the day.

Normal feeding behavior occurs exclusively at night so it is best to offer part of the daily diet after the lights have been turned off. Both flake and live foods are taken eagerly.

Newly acquired *Synodontis* catfish often require a period of adjustment to their new environment. The first two weeks are crucial in terms of acceptance or rejection of the new home. *Synodontis* unable to adapt succumb to any number of internal complications and quickly fade and die. Since these catfish have a bad habit of eating smaller fish in the aquarium, it is best to keep them only with fish too large to be eaten. With this type of arrangement, the catfish will normally keep to themselves and rarely disturb other fish in the tank. Little is known of the spawning behavior of Synodontis species. Up to now there have been only a few successful attempts at breeding *S. nignventris* in the aquarium .

Burkhard Kahl

(Top to bottom) Synodontis nummifer, Synodontis cf. nigrita, sold as the Nigerian lace cat.

Synodontis multipunctatus - A Cuckoo Among Catfishes

Reproduction by caffishes in aquaria is, with few exceptions, a relatively uncommon occurence. In light of this observations of the spawning behavior of *Synodontis multipunctatus,* a catfish endemic to Lake Tanganyika, are of great interest. Synodontis multipunctatus is an attractive species, popular with many keepers of Rift Lake cichlids. It is due largely to this popularity that information has come to light on the unusual reproductive behav-ior of this species. *Synodontis multipunctatus* practices a cuckoo-like style of brood parasitism. Spawning activity coincides with that of maternal mouthbrooding cichlids and is managed in such a fashion that the *Synodontis* eggs are picked up and brooded by the parental cichlid along with her own clutch. Many mouthbrooding cichlids will brood the eggs of other cichlid species under aquarium conditions. However, a relationship involving

The strikingly marked Tanganyikan Synodontis multipunctatus.
Photo: Burkhard Kahl

34

interspecific brooding of eggs between such divergent taxa is without precedent among fishes in nature or in captivity, it should be noted that the majority of the reported. *S multipunctatus* spawnings have utilized Lake Malawi cichlids as hosts. This state of affairs may at first seem strange, but in reality is not. While differences exist in the spawning behavior of maternal mouthbrooding cichlids, the patterns exhibited by Malawi and Tanganyikan species are sufficiently similar to explain the ease with the former have been adopted as surrogate hosts by *S. multipunctatus*. Aquarium spawnings involving two Tanganyikan species, *Tropheus duboisi* and *Cyphotilapia frontosa*, have also been reported.

Before discussing aquarium observations of this behavior, it is best to briefly review the history of this phenomenon. The noted collector Pierre Brichard first published (1979) an article noting that the

(Top to bottom) Riverine Synodontis, such as this S. velifer, are eggscatterers.
Photo: P. V. Loiselle
It remains to be seen if other Tanganyikan Synodontis, such as this S. petricola, are also brood-parasites.
Photo: P. V. Loiselle

35

Two S. multipunctatus breaking into the spawning sequence of a pair of the Malawian Pseudotropheus lombardoi Photo: Bruce Smith

The female catfish attempts to come between the female chichlid and her consort after a batch of eggs has been deposited but before they have been picked up. The male catfish is out of camera range. Photo: Bruce Smith

The female catfish attempts to eat as many cichlid eggs as she can while depositing a number of her own, which the female cichlid then takes into her mouth.
Photo: Bruce Smith

broods of a number of freshly captured parental females of several mouthbrooding Tanganyikan cichlids also contained fry of *S. multipunctatus*. Brichard theorized that young *Synodontis* swam into the mouths of brooding females while they slept. Observations have shown this theory to be incorrect. Rather, the presence of catfish in cichlid mouths has a far more fascinating explanation.

The first hints of this interesting situation appeared in 1978. Noted American aquarist James Langhammer (1978) briefly noted reports of an unidentified *Synodontis* being brooded by Cyphotilapia frontosa. Over the next five years verbal reports of cichlids brooding *S. multipunctatus* were heard from time to time. Odjik (1981) described a similar cuckoo relationship ostensibly involving the Malawian species *Synodontis njassae*. It seems probable the species in question was actually *S. multipunctatus*.

In 1983 the topic finally received good coverage with the publication of three reports (Ferguson, 1983; Finley, 1983; Koziol, 1983). Subsequently, Finley (1984) published a review article in corporating both new material and synopsis of previous reports.

Initially, spawnings of *S. multipunctatus* in the aquarium were noted when fry were released along with cichlid young or when found among the embryos of females stripped for artificial incubation. Some early reports (Rosen, pers. comm.) noted that prior to the discovery of *Synodontis* fry, adult catfish present in the aquarium had been seen attempting to "break up" the spawning act of the host cichlid. Subsequent observations revealed that "breaking in" or intervention to be a more appropriate term for such behavior

In an aquarium containing appropriate hosts and *S. multipunctatus*, catfish spawning is triggered by

The male cichlid reacts to this intrusion by attempting to expell the S. multipunctatus from the spawning site. Photo: Bruce Smith

the spawning activity of the cichlids. This is possibly due to the inadvertent release of chemical cues by the latter although visual clues may also play a role. All of the Synodontis present become involved. *S. multipunctatus* is a schooling species and is probably a natural group spawner. For optimum results, a group of *Synodontis* is best, but single pairs have also bred successfully in captivity. In good condition, *S. multipunctatus* can be easily sexed by the plumpness of the females and by the conspicuously pointed whitish genital papilla of the male. Females display as ovipositor, which is broader and not as well defined as the male's papilla. As the cichlids spawn, the *Synodontis* constantly intrude themselves into the spawning arena. With each pass through they lay and fertilize their own eggs while eating many of the cichlid's.

While this taking place the female cichlid invariably picks up some of the catfish eggs, not withstanding that they are quite different in appearance from her own. The eggs of *S. multipunctatus* are opaque white and about 1/3 of the size of a typical mbuna egg.

The *Synodontis* intervention continues throughout the spawning act. They may be chased by the cichlids but continually return to the arena to continue their spawning. *Synodontis* activity usually concludes once the cichlids have finished spawning.

Data are not available on the fecundity of *S. multipunctatus*. In the wild it has an extended breeding season, which suggests that smaller numbers of eggs are probably produced over an extended interval. No doubt more eggs are laid than picked up by the host cichlids. Under natural conditions, these would be left to take their chances for survival. This seems to be the case with the generality of *Synodontis* species, which are egg scatterers not known to practice parental care of the spawn. In captivity, these eggs are quickly eaten, although a rare one may survive. These observations are fascinating, but what follows the initial uptake of the catfish eggs is even more so. Recall there is already a reduction in the cichlid's brood size due to the number of eggs eaten during spawning by the *Synodontis*. Removal of the eggs from the mouth of parasitized female cichlid immediately after spawning and comparison of their contents with the number of eggs actually spawned demonstrates this. The number of *Synodontis* eggs present may vary. The largest number reported to date is 25. As natural incubation progresses fewer developing cichlid embryos are recovered. If the female is allowed to carry her clutch to full term, only *Synodontis* fry will be found. This situation results because while cichlid fry require c. three weeks to develop to independance, Synodontis fry

A male Cyphotilapia frontosa, one of the cichlids parasitized by S. multipunctatus in Lake Tanganyika. Photo: P. V. Loiselle

complete their development in 7 to 8 days. Once they reach this point, they will begin to use any cichlid embryos present as a food source! Observations made in "artificial mouths" have shown that the small *Synodontis* feed on cichlid embryos no larger than themselves but at a less advanced developmental stage This strategy is not without potential dangers to the *Synodontis* fry. Many held the normal developmental interval for their host emerge very emaciated, due to an inade-

quate food supply. Released by their host, the young *Synodontis* readily accept newly hatched brine shrimp as a first food. They grow rather rapidly, reaching 38 mm total length around 6 weeks post spawning. If one is confronted with a suspected spawning removing the brood a week or so after spawning will afford the *Synodontis* the best chance for survival.

The color pattern of the young *Synodontis* is quite different than that of adult fish. However, within 4 to

6 weeksthey become recognizable-facsimiles of their parents. The fin pattern through this interval of growth is black edged in white, as seen on the adults.

For a photographic sequence showing fry development, see Finley ('84). There is no doubt much more to be learned about the unique reproductive habits of *S. multipunctatus.*

Furthermore, the question of whether other Tanganyikan *Synodontis* share this reproductive startegy remains entirely open. Hopefully further study and observations by aquarists will resolve this issue.

Lee Finley

LITERATURE CITED

Brichard, P. 1979. Unusual brooding behaviors in Lake Tanganyika cichlids. *Buntbarsche Bull.* (74): 10 12.

Ferguson, J.1983, Observations of a spawning of *Synodontis multipunctatus* among Rift Lake cichlids. *Buntbarsche Bull.* (98): 13 - 16.

Finley, L. 1983. *Synodontis multipunctatus* reproduction and maternal mouthbrooding cichlids: a cuckoo relationship? *Buntbarsche Bull.* (98): 17 - 18.

Finley, L. 1984. Reproduction in *Synodontis multipunctatus. Freshwater and Marine Aquarium,* 7 (6): 22 25 et seg.

Koziol, T. J. 1983. Spawning an old friend, *Synodontis multipunctatus. All Cichlids,* 4 (2): 11 - 12 et seg.

Langhammer, J. K.1978. Mouthbrooders vs. Mouthbreeders. *Buntbarsche Bull.* (68): 28, 30.

Odjik, R. 1981. *Synodontis njassae* Keilhack 1908: a cuckoo among fishes. *Catfish Assoc. Gr Britain Mag.* (29): 8.

Above: Leocassius siamensis, Siamese bumblefee catfish
Below: Synodontis ocellifer Photos: P. V. Loiselle

"DEEP THROAT"
IN THE AQUARIUM

Purchasers of aquarium fish are lured by a variety of reasons - color, beauty, peronality or rarity to name just a few. Catfish acquisitions, however, are initially considered to be functional: scavangers, algae eaters, worker fish! However, the ever expanding variety of catfish seen in pet shops coincides with increased hobbyist interest in catfish as desirable aquarium residents in their own right. "They're so ugly, they're cute" would probably explain most sales of the angler catfish of the genus *Chaca*. These highly predatory soft skinned catfish have a variable blotched marble pattern. Random shades of light cacao to deep brown and black overlay a seemingly shapeless velvet body. The result: Perfect camouflage for the leaf litter and bog wood strewn stream bottoms where it lives.

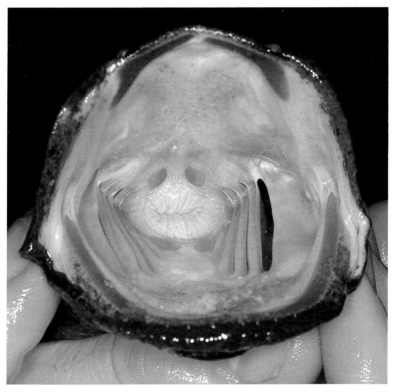

Chaca bankanensis showing the full gape of the jaws. Photo: Carl J. Ferraris, Jr.

No internal organs! That thought flashed into my mind the first time I saw a *Chaca* yawn. It looked like a funnel with a tail attached. The gape of the mouth is incredible. A specimen 20 cm (8") long has a mouth opening 10 cm (4") wide! The fins are miniscule, save for the powerful caudal fin which acts as both paddle and rudder.

During the daylight hours, this nocturnal gape and suck predator remains motionless. The small maxillary barbles are said to be used as "angling lures". Hence the common name of angler catfish. However, I have only seen this behavior once, in a very hungry, newly imported specimen. Lured by the worm-like motion of the barbles, a goldfish was literally inhaled by the powerful vacuum produced by the abrupt opening of the predator's mouth. *Chaca* was originally believed to be a monotypic genus. However, two species of this Asian catfish are currently recognized: *Chaca chaca* and *Chaca bankanensis*. The geographic districution of the two species does not overlap. The former is native to India and Burma, the latter to the Malay Peninsula and Indonesia. For the hobbyist the easiest way to distinguish between the two is to count the pectoral fin rays. *Chaca chaca* has five, *Chaca bankanensis* has four. The animals available in the hobby all appear to be *C. bankanensis*.

Mention "talking catfish" to a hobbyist and chances are he'll think of one of the South American doradid catfishes. Yet the generic name *Chaca* is derives from a Bengali word that alludes to similar sound production. Allegedly, when removed from the water, specimens "talk". *"Chaca ... Chaca ... Chaca"* sounds reputedly are rapidly emited. Although I have tried many times, I have never been able to elicit this response from any of my fish. Perhaps sound production is unique to *Chaca chaca*.

Definitely not community tank residents, these catfish should be purchased only by true enthusiasts. Captive maintenance requires a diet strictly of live food - lots of it! Contrary to my experience with other predator catfish, I have never been able to "train" *Chaca bankanensis* to accept anything else. Individuals 5 cm (2") long are quite capable of devouring guppies. At 10 cm (5") long, adults have no difficulty managing the largest feeder goldfish.

While maintaining a small group of these mighty mouths, I became aware of a strange penomenon. One afternoon I placed 20 feeder guppies in the angler cat's tank. Several hours later I noticed nearly all were dead. Amazed, I checked the feeder tank. Those guppies were fine. I removed the dead guppies from the *Chaca* tank and replaced them with live ones. That evening, I discoverd more dead guppies in the *Chaca* tank. I couldn't imagine what was going on. Upon reflection, I realized

Chaca bankanensis resting among fallen leaves. Photo: Carl J. Ferraris, Jr.

I had never previously put guppies in that tank and left the lights on. For the next few days I experimented. Guppies added to the tank during the day picked at the tank bottom and grazed on the *Chaca* in search of food. These guppies always died, I suggest there is a toxic substance in the body slime of *Chaca bankanensis* lethal to fish that ingest it.

Perhaps this unique defense mechanism is somehow related to the presence of a small pore at the base of the pectoral fin. The function of and secretions produced by the axillary gland to which it connects are unknown.

Interestingly, according to Weber and de Beaufort (in Roberts, 1982) in parts of Sumatra local people consider the flesh of *Chaca bankanensis* to be poisonous.

Although their diet is damanding, little else about this species. *Chaca*

bankanensis easily adapts to a wide range of water conditions. Like all aquarium residents, angler catfish require regular partial water changes to stay in good health. Their preferred substrate is fine sand. They like to burrow in it very much like the "banjo cats" of the family Bunocephalidae. Driftwood and leaves add to their comfort and security.

Catfish are the most under-rated of predators because they strike when the tank lights go out. They are usually the last to be considered by hobbyists as "culprits" in strange fish disappearances. Unlike other predatory members of the group *Chaca bankanensis* is tolerant of other catfish species not easily swallowed. I have kept three 18 cm (7") long *Chaca* in a 20 gallon tank with a 15 cm (6") long jaguar catfish *(Liosomadoras oncinus)*. The jaguar, previously a picky eater,

Frontal view of C. bankanensis. Photo: P.V. Loiselle

began voraciously eating goldfish while living with the *Chaca bankanensis.*

Large specimens are not always as tolerant of conspecifics. As they grow larger, captive individuals seem to become territorial. Males appear more given to interact aggressively with one another when crowded. The aggressive behavior is bizzare. Amazingly, initial confrontations often lead to lip-locking. It seems that the desirable position is to have control of the opponent's lower jaw. While jockeying for position, the confestants open their mouths to reveal an incredible gape. They seem to be attempting to swallow each other! Possibly to preclude such an outcome first one combatant, then the other will swell up to amazing proportions. They look like blow fish with posterior paddles. Interacting fish appear to be able to control the extend of this "swelling" quite precisely. The value of such an ability to control one's size in an altercation is obvious for such a highly evolved predator.

One might ask how to recognize a male *Chaca* without resort to surgery. Though the literature is silent on the subject, there is a clear color difference that distinguishes the sexes in *Chaca bankanensis.*

Of the first three *Chaca* I acquired, two had brown "camouflage" eyes and one had very distinctive white eyes. I assumed the white-eyed *Chaca* was blind. Since this didn't interfere with its ability to eat and grow. I never gave the matter much thought. Several years later I saw a wholesale shipment of several hundred small *Chaca bankanensis.* Alsmost half had white eyes. I certainly don't believe that half the *Chaca* in the wild are blind. Based upon girth (of adult specimens) and behavior, I now believe that white-eyed individuals are females, dark-eyed individuals males.

Nothing is known about the reproductive mode of either *Chaca* species. Dissection of a large 20 cm long (10"), obviously gravid female *Chaca bankanensis* that died suddenly in my tank revealed well-developed ovaries. Eggs of several sizes were present, the largest measuring 6.5 mm in diameter, the smallest 3.0 mm in diameter. This suggestes the possibility of several spawnings in a given season. A much smaller female, only 10 cm (5") long, was subsequently also found to contain an active ovary. Despite many years of serching and an investment of thousands of goldfish; I have yet to find the right "trigger" to induce the *Chaca* to spawn in captivity. I intend to continue trying, although I shudder to think of the food requirements of a whole spawn of baby angler catfish!

Ginny Eckstein

LITERATURE CITED

Roberts, Tyson R., 1982, A Revision of the South and Southeast Asian Angler Catfishes (Chacidae).

PELAGIC CATFISHES

Catfishes are usually thought of as rather sedentary, bottom-living organisms.

Most of the families that make up the enormous suborder Siluroidei conform well enough to this stereotype. However, three Neotropical (Ageniosidae, Auchenipteridae and Hypopthalmidae) and three Old World (Siluriade, Schilbeidae and Pangasiidae) catfish families deviate dramatically from this popular image. Most or all of their constituent species are active, midwater-living fish whose pelagic life-style allows them to exploit zooplankton or small schooling fishes for food. Ageniosids are large, fast-swimming occasionally imported pursuit prdators sold under the common name of gulper catfish. There are three recognized hypopthalmid species. All are specialized plankton feeders. None has ever been imported as an aquarium fish. Several pelagic auchenipterids are sporadically available to aquarists. Their husbandry is the subject of a separate chapter by Dr. Carl Ferraris. This essay will focus on the representatives of the three Old-World families commonly kept as aquarium fish.

Although they differ considerably among themselves in adult size, feeding patterns and general level of compatibility with other fishes, these pelagic catfishes share several critical maintenance requirements. First and foremost, all are schooling fishes. Like other highly social animals, they feel comfortable only when kept in groups of their own kind. Isolated specimens either hide all the time or else engage in panicky flight at the slightest disturbance. During the course of these frantic dashes to and fro, the fish often collide with the tank walls and furnishings, doing themselves serious injury. Alternatively, they leap from the tank onto the floor, with predictable consequences. To see these catfish at their best, always keep them in schools of at least a half dozen individuals.

Secondly, these fish require plenty of swimming room. The smaller schilbeids and silurids should never be kept in tanks smaller than 20 gallos (c. 80 l) capacity, while 30 gallons (c. 120 l) comes far closer to providing them with adequate living conditions. Adults of the larger schilbeids and pangasiids need at least 6' (c. 2.0 m) of swimming room to prosper. Aquarists who cannot meet these admitedly generous requirements should turn their attention to more sedentary catfishes. Few sights are more depressing than a large pelagic catfish housed in a tank that requires it to constantly retrace a circular path whose diameter barely exceeds its own length.

The Nigerian flagtail catfish, Eutropiella buffei. Photo: P.V. Loiselle

Finally, these catfish hail from riverine habitats characterized by moderate to swift currents. Like most inhabitants of such biotopes, they have little tolerance of dissolved ammonia or nitrite. Careful nitrogen cycle management is thus an essential adjunct to their successful maintenance. Efficient biological filtration combined with frequent partial water changes will keep them in vigorous health. Fortunately, these catfish prosper over a wide range of pH and hardness conditions. This greatly simplifies carrying out regular partial water changes in their tanks. They are more sensitive to dissolved chlorine than most other catfish, however. Hence it is prudent to treat fresh water destined for their tank with Tetra's Contra Chlorine + and Aqua-Safe to minimize the possibility of accidental skin and gill damage when making water changes. If the municipal water supply is chloramine treated, it is essential to use a dechlorination agent in conjunction with a chemically active filter medium such as PolyBio-Marine's PolyFilterRR to prevent losses at this time.

The Family Schilbeidae is found in both Africa and tropical Asia. Two species of Nigerian provenance are commonly available to aquarists. *Schilbe mystus,* usually sold under the trade name of grasscutter cat, is a vigorous species known to attain 16" (c. 40.0 cm) standard length.

The glass catfish, Physailia pellucida, is the most popular representative of this group. Photo: K. Paysan

Its overall shape is reminiscent of a machete blade, hence its common name, based upon the West African pidgin word for this all-purpose implement! Junvenile *Schilde* are strikingly marked with parallel steel-blue stripes on a silvery grey background. As they grow older, the contrast between stripes and background diminishes markedly, though a dark shoulder spot always remains conspicuous.

Similarly colored representatives of the genus *Eutropius* are sometimes found in shipments of fish from Nigeria or Zaire. They can be easily recognized by the presence of an adipose fin. An attractively blotched congener, *Schilde marmoratus,* is sometimes exported from Zaire. These occasional imports should be treated in the same manner as *S. mystus.* Grasscutter cats are highly social omnivores with strong predatory tendencies and voracious appetites. Stranded insects, grass seeds, fruit and fish up to a third their overall length comprise their menu in nature. Bear this in mind when selecting their tankmates! In captivity, all the usual prepared and live foods are devoured with gusto. Pelletized foods such as Tetra's Doro-Min provide a convenient and nutritionally satisfacotory staple diet for this and other large pelagic catfish. Juvenile *Schilbe* will eat until their stomachs are perfectly sperical, then show no trace of their enormous meal a few hours later. Needless to say, they grow very rapidly. As they will leap out of the water in an attempt to capture insects that fly overhead, a tight cover is absolutely essential for their tank. There are no reports of captive spawing by either *Schilbe* or *Eutropius.*

The Nigerian flagtail catfish, *Eutropiella beiffei,* is an extremely attractive schilbeid that rarely exceeds 10.0 cm (c. 4") overall length. It is frequently - though mistakenly - sold and written about under the name *E. debauwi,* a valid but less frequently exported Zairean species that lacks the dark spots in the caudal fin lobes. These diminutive schilbeids are excellent community residents. A school of six to eight individuals makes a particularly attractive display in a planted aquarium.

In nature, *E. buffei* feeds upon zooplankton and small stranded terrestrial insects. In captivity, flake, freeze-dried, fresh frozen and live foods of appropriate size are eagerly eaten. The Nigerian flagtail cat is an egg-scatterer whose spawning in nature is linked to the onset of the rainy season. There are several reports of unplanned spawnings by well-fed groups of this species in captivity. The resulting fry were easily reared on a diet of microworms, *Artemia nauplii* and finely powdered prepared foods. This suggests *E. buffei* would profitably repay the attentions of serious fish breeders.

The Family Siluridae is native to both temperature and tropical Eurasia. It includes a number of giant predators, such as the wels, or European catfish, *Silurus glanis,* which can grow to 5.0 m (c. 15') in length, and the helicopter catfish, *Wallago attu,* a southeast Asian species that can reach a length of 2.0 m (c. 6'). Without a doubt, the group's most popular representative is the aptly named glass catfish, *Kryptopterus bicirrhus.* Native to Sumatra, Jawa and Borneo, this striking plankton feeder grows to 10.0 cm (c. 4 inches) SL, although specimens offered for sale are typically half this size. Its delicate appearance notwithstanding, *K. bicirrhus* is a surprisingly hardy little fish. It readily devours any live or prepared foods small enough to be easily taken and prospers over a wide range of water conditions. The glass catfish is an excellent community resident. However, take care not to house it with aggressive companions. This is an easily bullied species that reacts to persecution by hiding. Surprisingly enough in view of its long history as an aquarium resident and considerable popularity, nothing is known of the reproductive biology of *K. bicirrhus.* There are no reports of aquarium spawnings, aquarists remaining dependant upon imported specimens from Singapore. The genus comprises several larger, less transparent species that are sometimes confused with representatives of the genus *Ompok.* The dorsal fin in the

The irridescent shark, Pangasius sutchii, a large pelagic catfish.

Photo: P.V. Loiselle

latter genus, while small, still contains several distinct rays, in contradistinction to the single-spined dorsal fin of *Kryptopterus*. These false glass cats can grow as large as 60.0 cm (c. 2') in length. They will prey upon smaller fishes, a fact to keep in mind when selecting their tankmates. Two dwarf African schilbeid genera are also sufficiently transparent to have warranted the name of glass catfish. They differ from *Kryptopterus* in having three rather than two pairs of barbels and species-specific patterns of fine black dots in the flanks. Representatives of the genus *Physailia* have a diminutive adipose but no dorsal fin. Those of the genus *Parailia* lack

both dorsal and adipose fins. Both African glass catfish should be treated in the same manner as *K. bicirrhus.*

The Family Pangasidae is restricted to the freshwaters of India and Southeast Asia. It too includes some real behemoths, among them *Pangasiodon gigas,* a huge plankton-feeding catfish endemic to hte Mekong River system that can attain weights up to 300 kg. The species most widely available to aquarists, *Pangasius sutchii,* is a Thai species that can exceed a meter (c. 3') in length under favorable conditions. Sold under the trade names of irridescent shark or Asian shark cat, it is an important food fish in Thailand, where fingerlings are produced by the thousands for pond stocking. This is the source of the juvenile and subadult specimens imported for the ornamental fish trade. This almost industrial production of fry doubtless favored the development of the very attractive albino color variety of this species frequently offered for sale to aquarists.

The irridescent shark has much the same feeding habits in nature as do *Schilbe,* and should be handled in the same fashion in captivity. Notwithstanding its fearsome name, *P. sutchii* is less predatory under aquarium conditions than is its African analog. It does, however, require more swimming room and water movement than the grasscutter cat, whose proclivity for jumping it fully shares. A tight-fitting, heavily weighted cover is essential, for large specimens are powerful enough to knock an unweighted cover glass askew in their efforts to exit their tank. Though it is regularly bred under pond conditions, there are no reports of aquarium spawnings of *P. sutchii.* The large adult size of the irridescent shark as much as any other factor largely precludes the possibility of such an accomplishment anywhere outside the facilities of a public aquarium. Their unusual morphology and outgoing behavior doubtless explain the continuing popularity of these pelagic catfishes.

The peculiarities of their life style dictate that they be treated somewhat differently than the generality of catfishes. However, as long as their needs for adequate living space and clean, well aerated water are met, these non-confirmist catfish are a welcome addition to any aquarium.

Dr. P.V. Loiselle

and sport fishes. *Ictalurus punctatus,* the channel catfish, is a frequent target for anglers. It is so highly prized as a food fish that it is regularly on the menu of most restaurants in southeastern United States. Throughout the region, catfish farming is an impoertant commercial enterprise. With catfish culture being practiced on such a grand scale, it is not surprising to find that an albino cultivated variety has been developed. The albino channel catfish is regularly marketed throught the pet trade. With the resurgence of interest among aquarists in native cold water fish, it is similarly not surprising to find normally-pigmented channel catfish being sold beside their albino cousins in many pet stores.

Though readily available to the amateur aquarist, channel catfish are not the most aquaristically desirable members of the family. Their chief drawback is their size. Given

Juvenile albino channel catfish are better suited to aquarium life than are adults.
Photo: P.V. Loiselle
A subadult specimen of the normal color form of the channel catfish.
Photo: William R. Kenney

Fully grown albino channel catfish, Ictalurus punctatus. Photo: P.V. Loiselle

their healthy appetites and a year-round growing season, they quickly attain lengths in excess of 50.0 cm (20"). Such a fish places heavy demands on almost anyone's available tank space.

Channel cats voraciously consume all the normal aquarium fare suited to large fish with healthy appetites. Their diet will inevitably include any tankmates small enough to fit their capacious mouths, for after dark becomes this species like any other ictalurid, an extremely effective predator. The only solution to this problem is to exclude from the aquarium any fish small enough to become prey. The choice of potential tankmates large enough to escape the attentions of a half-meter (20") long catfish, is limited. For aquarists interested in maintaining ictalurids a more palatable approach is to work with a smaller species. Whereas the fork-tailed *Ictalurus* species all grow quite large, the square-tailed species formerly placed in the separate genus, *Ameiurus,* collectively known as bullheads, offer a more attractive alternative. These typically attain an adult size of 30 cm (1') under aquarium conditions. They can thus be housed comfortably in a tank of 100 liters (25 gallons) capacity or more. Aquaristically noteworthy species are the previously mentioned *Ictalurus nebulosus,* the slightly smaller *Ictalurus melas,* the black bullhead, an abundant species in central United States and one successfully established in Europe, and the attractive *Ictalurus natalis,* the yellow bullhead.

55

The black bullhead, Ictalurus melas, has been successfully if controversially naturalized in several European countries.

Even bullheads' tankmates must be selected with care, for only their capacity to devour other fish is constrained by their size, not their appetites! For the aquarist with even less tank space, or less tolerance for ictalurid predation, a still more attractive choice are the catfish of the genus *Noturus,* collectively known as madtoms. Although one species of this genus does reach 25 cm (10") standard length, most do not exceed half that length. This does not prevent them from becoming dangerous predators upon very small aquarium fishes. However, it does substantially restrict their choice of prey items, and thus gives the aquarist a broader choice of safe tankmates. Many *Noturus* species are attractively patterned, e.g., *Noturus albater,* the

ozark madtom, or *Noturus flavater,* the checkered madtom. These have color pattern reminiscent of the popular bumblebee catfishes.

Ictalurids are hardy aquarium residents. They do not appreciate extremely acid or alkaline water, but are otherwise indifferent to its pH and hardness. Bullheads have a considerable tolerance for polluted water, but both the fork-tailed *Ictalurus* species and the madtoms are quite sensitive to ammonia and nitrite. A program of regular partial water changes is essential to their successful maintenance. Though they can tolerate temperatures up to 30°C (85°F) *Ictalurus* species are best maintained at lower temperatures. They are less prone to disease when kept between 18 and 24°C (c. 65° to 75°F). Equally important, they eat

The yellow bullhead, Ictalurus natalis, another widely distributed North American catfish. Photo: Willian R. Kenney

much less in cooler water. Madtoms are typically riffle-dwellers whose tolerance for warm water is correspondingly less than that of their larger relatives. The temperature in their tanks should not be allowed to exceed 24°C (75°F). Although they will survive without a winter resting period, ictalurids are unlikely to experience normal gonadal development unless exposed to water temperatures below 10°C (c. 50°F) for a few months each year. Ictalurid catfishes spawn in the spring. A period of exposure to lower water temperature appears to be a prerequisite of normal reproductive activity in these catfish. However, aquarists willing to provide their fish with a winter rest interval experience few problems in inducing the smaller ictalurids to spawn in captivity.

The clutch is usually placed under the shadow of some structure such as submerged plank. The male guards and cleans the developing zygotes and continues to protect the newly mobile fry. He abandons the brood within a few days of hatching. Shortly thereafter, the swarm of fry can be seen as a conspicuous black formation swimming at the surface.

There are cases reported in which both parents played a custodial role, notably among the several bullhead species.

Adult ictalurids usually hide in thick cover during the day. They are thus not readily collected by the aquarist armed only with a small seine. A more effective approach to augmenting one's catfish collection is to watch for fry swarms in the spring and dip as many as needed from the school. This affords aquarists unable to meet the necessary conditions for spawning them in captivity the best opportunity to experience the pleasure of raising rearing ictalurid fry.

The tadpole madtom, Noturus gyrinus, is one of the commonest representatives of the genus. Photo: William R. Kenney
The envenomed spines of the margined madtom, Noturus insignis, can inflict extremely painful wounds. Photo: William R. Kenney

Occasionally juvenile madtoms may be collected from a school of bullhead fry. However, the aquarist wishes to collect adult madtoms should carefully inspect the discarded beverage cans found all too often in our waterways. Madtoms find these quite acceptable shelters! This method of collecting hardly yields fish in commercial quantities but on one occasion I found a male guarding a clutch of eggs in such a container.

When handling any catfish, be careful of the pectoral and dorsal fin spines.

The barbels, often though thought dangerous, are harmless. In most species of catfish thus far encountered, the degree of pain produced by spine punctures is far out of proportion to the amount of tissue damage resulting from such a wound. The inference is that venom is at work, whose virulence varies from species to species.

The slender madtom, Noturus exilis, is one of the larger madtom species. Photo: P.V. Loiselle

Not withstanding their small size, madtoms seem to produce the most painful wounds of all North American catfish. Handled gently, however, catfish spines are unlikely to penetrate the skin. Before collecting any native fish for aquarium use, consult relevant local game laws, and become familiar with any rare, threatened, or endangered species like to be found locally. Ignorance of the law is not an acceptable defense, while penalties for the capture of protected species can be severe, extending at judicial discretion, to confiscation of all vehicles and equipment employed by the guilty party or parties.

William R. Kenney

Page 60/61: Corydoras spec. Photo: B. Kahl ▶

GIANT PREDATORY CATFISH

An engaging feature of catfish is their wide variation in size. Aquarists can choose from a selection that spans a size range of c. 1.5 cm (1/2") to almost 5.0 m (16') overall length! Most aquarium catfishes happily fall between these extremes. The most widely kept species measure less than 10.0 cm (5") overall length. However, there are popular catfish which reach a considerably greater size in captivity. The management of these larger catfish is the subject of this article. Specifically, I will discuss representatives of three families: Ariidae, Bagridae and Pimelodidae. Although these families differ considerably in morphology, they share a common feature: all are naked (smooth-skinned) catfishes.

Before considering individual species of interest, it is worthwhile to discuss the maintenance of large catfishes in captivity. The primary consideration influencing their well-being is tank size. In order to maintain large catfishes successfully large aquaria are essential. Most of these fish are powerful and active swimmers that should never be housed in tanks shorter than twice their adult length. Bear in mind that most large species are initially

The red tail catfish, Practocephalus hemioliopterus, is a highly sought-after giant predatory species from South America. Photo: P.V. Loiselle

Adult shark catfish, Arias cf. jordani. Photo: P.V. Loiselle

available as juveniles. However, these will grow the often very rapidly! Ascertain from literature or by direct inquiry from other aquarists with prior experience of a particular species how large it will grow and select its tank accordingly. Certainly aquarists are limited in the size of the aquaria they can resonably maintain. But anyone wishing to keep such large fishes must be ready to go that proverbial "extra mile" to meet their space requirements. Good intention not withstanding a 60 cm (2') long catfish will not prosper if stuffed in a meter (3') long tank!

Large catfishes are powerful and accomplished jumpers. A well secured cover for their aquarium is an absolute necessity. Equally important to their successful maintenance is proper filtration. Filtration approaches appropriate to a large tank housing smaller fishes will usually prove inadequate for the same tank housing a large catfish. There are several workable approaches to filtration in a large catfish tank.

Mechanical filtration with a high volume power filter is the one most commonly used. Such units must have their media cleaned or replaced regularly to perform well. As large catfish can be messy tank residents, re-usable media are a good investment for their filters. Remember when using an outside power filter in a large catfish tank that it is wise to provide protection for the intake siphons. The fish often become "playful" or act aggressively towards intrusive and accessible objects. This can result in the interruption of filtration and aeration, with devastating consequences. Heaters also warrant some sort of protection. Most are fairly fragile objects that will not stand up to physical abuse by a large catfish. The easiest way to protect appliances in the large catfish tank is to partition off a zone 10 cm (5 inches) wide at the end of the tank with plastic "egg crate" diffuser grating. Heaters and siphons positioned behind this barrier are safe from catfish molestation.

Another filtration option relies on canister filters. Such units offer effective mechanical filtration as well as considerable biological activity if some care is taken in the selection of the media with which they are charged. As they do not rely upon siphon action to function they are also effectively catfish proof! Undergravel filtration in conjunction with an outside power filter is a third alternative. It works well only if the catfish in question doesn't dig extensively. However, where the fishes's behavior does not prohibit its use, such a dual system greatly aids in maintaining a successful catfish aquarium. Regardless of the filtration system one selects, a regular schedule of partial water changes is an essential feature of good catfish husbandry. Big fishes equal a big waste load. Only

The peruno cat, Perunichthys peruno, is one of the more commonly available of the giant predatory catfish. Photo: AquaLife Magazine/Japan

A juvenile marbled sailfin cat, Leiarius pictus. This strikingly marked pimelodid can be easily taught to take food from its keeper's hand.
Photo: Vince Edmundson

with proper filtration and regular water changes can a healthy environment for these fishes be maintained.

Another important fact of large catfish culture intimately connected with filtration and water changes is feeding. Proper feeding of large catfishes entails considerably more than just sprinkling flakes into the aquarium. These large catfish are all predatory to a greater or lesser degree, a fact to be considered when choosing their tankmates. While all benefit from the inclusion of live fish in their diet, they quickly learn to take such non-living items as strips of raw fish or lean meat, frozen or freeze-dried plankton and pelletized foods. To get the maximum benefit from offerings of live fish, keep them well fed. It is always a good idea to offer feeder fish a large meal of flake foods or brine shrimp before presenting them to any of those large catfish. Turning feeders into living vitamin pills is a painless way of adding nutritional supplements to any predator's diet. These fish tend to have large appetites. Most quickly come to associate their keeper with the arrival of food and often become adept beggars. Remember that satisfying such heathy appetites generates a substantial waste load and scale water changes in large catfish tanks accordingly.

It is important to choose potential tankmates for these large catfish carefully. While most would not be classified as "nasty" they definitely consider smaller tankmates a potential meal. Choose their companions with this in mind. Territorality must also be considered when

65

The tiger shovelnose cat, Pseudoplatystoma tigrinum, is more skittish in captivity than most large pimelodids. Photo: P.V. Loiselle

choosing potential tankmates. Many larger catfishes are strongly territorial and will not tolerate tankmates of any sort. Finding this out can sometimes be an expensive proposition. Devoting an entire aquarium to a single large catfish may seem an extravagent and inefficient use of tank space. However, such isolated specimens tend to interact with their keepers to a far greater degree than those kept in a community setting. Consequently, housing a large catfish alone can lead to a rewarding outcome - a bewhiskered "pet" in the true sense of the word. Although few members of the family Ariidae are commonly maintained in captivity, at least one species, which will attain a large size, is generally available. this family contains c. 130 species distributed among 20 - odd genera. Most ariids are marine fish, although a number of fresh water species are known. Even many "marine" species pass part of their lives in brackish and fresh water. The Ariidae have worldwide distribution in tropical and subtropical coastal waters. The Australia/New Guinea region boasts the largest number of fresh water species as well as the greates overall species diversity. Adult size varies. The largest species reach over one meter (3') in length. The species available to aquarists can grow to at least 30 to 45 cm (12" to 18"). Correctly identifying ariids is difficult because of the great similarity between species and the fact that marked physical changes occur as individuals grow.

This complicates the task of identifying the *Arius* species imported from Columbia. These fish are sold as tricolor cats, shark cats, or Columbian shark cats. Three species, *Arius jordani, Arius seemani* and *Arius felis* occur in this area which makes it difficult to correctly identify the fish available to hobbyists. I suggest either referring to these fish as *Arius* sp. or using one of the available common names. Most of the shark cats are 5.0 to 7.5 cm (2" to 3") long when imported. Their body color is silvery blue-grey with white-trimmed black fins. Their three pairs of barbles are dark. Mortalities during shipping and holding are high. However, once established in a home aquarium shark cats generally do well. The pH is not critical but is best kept neutral to slightly alkaline. The addition of salt is appreciated but not a necessity.

Ariids are opportunistic omnivores. Simply put, they will eat whatever comes their way! Feeding them is thus a simple matter. Ariids will devour other fishes enthusiastically. Small fish are eaten whole, lar-

(T. to b.) The true shovelnose cat, Sorubim lima, is less belligerent towards other catfishes than the other robust pimelodids discussed herein. Photo: B. Kahl
Goeldiella equens is a mid-sized pimelodid sometimes confusesd with the similarly colored but much less predatory zaireian bagrid catfish Chrysichthys marmoratus. Photo: P.V. Loiselle

Representatives of the genus Rhamdia are among the few pimeloid catfish native to Central America. Photo: P.V. Loiselle

ger individuals literally torn into pieces, then eaten. As these catfish grow rapidly to over 60.0 cm (2') long, this behavior must be kept in mind when selecting their tankmates. All three Columbian ariids are paternal mouthbrooders, but there are no accounts of successful breeding in captivity.

The Central and South American family Pimelodidae contains many interesting and attractive large catfish among its c. 300 known species. Many of these can truly become "pets" and develop a relationship with their keepers. Pimelodids vary greatly in adult size. The smaller species barely reach 5.0 cm (2") standard length while the giants of the family, such as *Brachyplatystoma filamentosum,* may approach 3.0 meters (9') in length. All, regardless of size, are efficient predators with large mouths as standard equipment. Keep this in mind when choosing potential tankmates. Many are also territorial, and which may make it difficult to keep other fishes with tehm. Maintenance pre-

sents no problems. A varied, meaty diet, good filtration and frequent water changes will keep them happy. Some species, especially *Pseudoplatystoma,* initially tend to be a little jumpy. It is thus best to avoid startling them. I've seen a 25 cm (10 inch) tiger shovelnose crack its tank's end panel after a sudden movement startled it into panicked flight.

Phractocephalus hemioliopterus, the South American red-tailed catfish, is one of the most stunning of the large pimelodids. Its distinctive shape and diagnostic color pattern have made it a favorite of aquarists for years. In the wild this species can exceed 2.0 meter (6.6') in length but such a size is not to be expected in captivity. Although it may be successfully maintained on a diet of smaller fishes and meaty foods, gut studies on wild fish show that they consume a fair amount of vegetable material, such as palm fruits. Fresh water crabs are also commonly taken by wild specimens! Attempts to similarly broa-

Pimelodus clarias will eat smaller fishes, but as it rarely exceeds 30.0 cm overall length, it is safer community tank risk than its larger relatives.

Photo: P.V. Loiselle

Pimelodus pictus, often sold under the trade name "Pimelodus angelicus", is a popular member of the family Pimelodidae. Photo: P.V. Loiselle

Pimelodus cf. albafasciatus, another frequently imported small pimelodid catfish. Photo: P.V. Loiselle

Easily confused with juvenile jelly catfish, the South American bumblebee cat, Microglanis iheringi, never exceeds 8.0 cm overall length. Phtoto: P.V. Loiselle

Adult giraffe catfish, Auchenoglanis occidentalis, can grow up to a meter long.
Photo: Lee Finley

Although it only grows to 30.0 cm overall length, the jelly or frog catfish, Pseudo-pimelodus raninus is a voracious predator.

Above: The Asian bumblebee cats, such as Leocassis poeciliopterus, are members of the family Bagridae.
Right: The smaller Parauchenoglanis guttatus rarely exceeds 20.0 cm overall
length. Photo: P.V. Loiselle

den the diets of aquarium-held specimens are thus to be encouraged. Feeding this and other large catfish need not be a daily affair. After a large meal, a number of days may pass before food need to be offered them again. *Perrunichthys perruno* is one of the more commonly available of the large pimelodids. An attractive color pattern coupled with the extremely long maxillary (upper jaw) barbles makes this species indeed distinctive. Native to northern South America, *P. perruno* is known to exceed 60 cm (2') in length in the wild. given proper care and room it will easily attain this size in captivity. Like the redtailed catfish, this species will learn to recognize, an become receptive, to its owner. Once this tage is reached, the result is a large catfish that will "beg" for food and can be fed by hand.

The Asian red tail catfish, Mystus nemurus, is a formidable predator.
Photo: P.V. Loiselle

Leiarius pictus is superficially similar to the preceeding species, both physically and behaviorably. Its body is less flattened than that of *Perunichthys* and its dorsal fin is larger. This last feature is responsible for its common names of sailfin cat and sailfin "perruno". The light stripe which begins at the dorsal fin origin and curves down and back to the caudal peduncle, is unfailingly diagnostic of this species.

Leiarius has the same maintenance requirements as *Perrunichthys*. Like the forgoing species, it also has considerable potential as a "pet" fish. The sail-fin cat is less commonly available and usually more expensive than *P. perruno,* but is definitely worth the greater investment. Medium sized specimens c.

30 cm (1') in length are usually exported, but on rare occasions, juveniles, less than 20 cm (8") in length are available. These are particularly attractive and definitely worth obtaining.

Catfish of the genus *Pseudoplatystoma,* commonly known as tiger shovelnose, are popular and generally available. Two species, *P. fasciatum* and *P. tigrinum* are seen in the hobby. *P. fasicatum* is the more commonly available of the two. It typically shows thin dark vertical bars as opposed to the more reticulated pattern of *P. tigrinum.* These species, although distinctive and eye catching, rarely become as tame as the preceeding three. Even after a considerable time in captivity, they tend to remain a little "spoo-

A mid-sized bagrid catfish from India, Mystus vittatus. Photo: P.V. Loiselle

ky". The presence of functional decoration, such as large pieces of driftwood, in their tank can help to keep them a little calmer. Be sure not to turn the tank lights on suddenly when the surrounding area is in the dark. This can startle them badly and make them dash about frantically, causing harm to themselves and the tank equipment.

The large African and Asian family Bagridae contains at least 200 species. As with the pimelodids, most available as aquarium residents are small, but a few large species are sporadically available to hobbyists. Two species, one African and one Asian, deserve particular mention here.

Auchenoglanis occidentalis is an African species with an elongate snout and an attractive color pattern. Commonly known as the giraffe-nosed catfish, it is truly a prize and definitely of the most interesting larger catfishes. Known to reach lengths in excess of a meter (3') in the wild, it will approach this size in captivity if well fed and housed.

Like many larger catfishes, this species is usually available to aquarists at a small size. The color pattern in jeveniles under 20 cm (8") in length is much crisper than that of adults. As individuals grow, their color pattern softens but the overall effect still makes for a very attractive fish.

Although it will eat smaller fish when it can, this species consumes a more diverse diet in nature. It is easily maintained on a diet of meaty fresh foods an pellets in captivity.

Auchenoglanis are also bottom sifters. They can routinely be observed ingesting large amounts of gravel after removing any food particles, expelling it from their gill covers. This activity makes the use of undergravel filtration of questionable value with this species. Either an outside power or canister

The two-spot catfish, Mystus micracanthus, grows to c. 10.0 cm total length. The small size of this Malaysian bagrid recommends it for the community tank.
Photo: P.V. Loiselle

filter should be used on its tank. *Mystus nemurus* is commonly known as the Asian red tail catfish. This elongate Southeast Asian species has a grayish body and a caudal fin that ranges from deep yellow to red in color. It is superficially similar to a number of pimelodids but can be quickly distinguished by the presence of a fourth pair of barbles, the nasals. *M. nemurus* is usually imported on the 10.0 to 20.0 cm (5" to 8") size range. When provided with a large aquarium and good care it will easily grow three times longer in captivity. Maximum size known in nature is somewhat in excess of 60.0 cm (2') in length. *M. nemurus* is quite predatory and relishes a diet of small fishes. It will also accept fresh meaty and pelleti-zed food. This species can be very territorial. Larger specimens may be very difficult to maintain with other fishes. Kept alone, it usually becomes very tame and makes a good pet. But even well adapted individuals always remain a bit nervous. Given its skill as a jumper, this makes a full and solidly weighted cover on its aquarium a necessity.

In closing, I would say that if you like larger fishes, do consider some of these catfishes. This article barely scratches the surface of available species and is meant only as a brief introduction to this fascinating group of animals. The enjoyment to be derived from keeping these giant predators is almost unlimited.

Lee Finley

THE BANJO CATFISH

I met my first banjo catfish, *Buno-cephalus* sp., under very strange circumstances a few years back. I already had experience of keeping other species of catfish, but this one was new to me. As I am especially fond of the aquatic plants belonging to the genus *Cryptocoryne*, I paid a visit to a local pet shop to purchase some of these interesting aquatic plants. After choosing the specimens I wanted, the dealer removed them from the tank and began to pack them up for me. It was then that I noticed something brown on one of the leaves, and on closer examination it turned out to be a banjo catfish about 4 cm long. As these fish are very rarely offered for sale in pet shops, I was more than willing to accept it! The only problem was that the dealer was reluctant to let me have it for nothing, but after a short friendly discussion, I agreed with the dealer to purchase a second *Bunocephalus* if he would let me have the first one free! Thus I ended up with the *Cryptocoryne* species that I had intended to purchase, and two fine specimens of an unusual catfish. I introduced these fish into one of my 100 litre aquaria which already housed a few wild-type swordtails, and they both immediately vanished into the dense vegetation and lava-stone formations. For the next two weeks I did not see them at all,

but I was not particularly surprises at this, as I already knew that the banjo catfish preferred the cover of darkness. I provided a wide variety of food for my fish, and one evening when I put some TetraMin Tablets into the tank, the catfish appeared for the first time. Almost before the tablets reached the bottom, the two *Bunocephalus* emerged from their hiding places and headed straight for the food with their characteristic jerky swimming motion. However, they didn't stay for long, but grabbed a tablet with their mouths and headed back for cover, not be seen again for days. Some time later I had to thin out the profuse growth of *Crypto-coryne*, and it was then that I discovered just where the catfish were hiding. They had manged to secrete themselves into tiny crevices that were only just large enough to take them, and it appeared that each fish had its own particular crevice that it kept to itself.

This *Bunocephalus* species (one of several) lives in running water in the Amazon region of South America, is omnivorous, and attains a body length of 6-8 cm. The fish are of a basic brown colour with irregular light brown spots. They have two pairs of barbels, the shorter pair, about 0.5 cm long, are located on the lower jaw, whilst the longer pair, about 1-2 cm, protrude from

Banjo catfish, Bunocephalus spec. Photo: Dr. W. Foersch

the upper jaw. The head and anterior part of the body is considerably flattened, but the tail is narrow and roud, giving an overall shape not unlike that of a "banjo" - hence the name banjo catfish. The pectoral fins are very large in relation to the body size, and are spread out at right angles to the body (both when at rest and when moving forward). This species of catfish has difficulty swimming about in open water, and always rests with its body lying on something. The body is also covered with small hooks which enable it to anchor itself to stones and plants. The eyes are extremely small, each about the size of a pin head, indicating relatively poor sight. This is perhaps not unexpected in a nocturnal fish. In keeping with the habitat from which they originate, banjo catfish prefer fairly soft water, but they nevertheless grow to a ripe old age in medium hard aquarium water at a temperature of 25°C. Very little is known about the breeding requirements of this species, and in fact it is even difficult to distinguish between the sexes. My two banjo catfish that I acquired in such an unusual way have been swimming around (or rather lying around!) in my aquarium now for about six years, and I have learned a lot about their strange and interesting living habits. After all this time I know that I would not like to be without them in my collection, and would recommend them as a welcome addition to any aquarist's stock of fish who appreciates something a little out of the ordinary!

Lothar Wischnath

A SPAWNING
OF THE BANJO CATFISH

I found the contribution on the frying pan catfish *(Bunocephalus* spp.), a fish widely distributed in the region east of the Andes in South America, in a recent edition of the Aquarium digest International very interesting, as I keep a number of them in my 100 litre tank. However, to contradict the view stated in that article, I must say that I have found sex differentiation is quite straightforward. The females are somewhat larger than the males, and a spawning time their huge girth is very noticeable. On 26 October 1980 I even had an opportunity of observing their spawning behaviour.

It is a well known fact that these catfish burrow into the substrate during the day and only become active in search of food as darkness approaches. On this particular occasion, having switched off the lights before going to bed, I could see that the fish had emerged from their hideaways and one of the males was probing the females belly with his barbels. After this the pair entwined themselves and circled around each other with a jerky motion. The whole procedure lasted about a minute. The female then disappeared under a bogwood root, carrying some yellowish eggs between her ventral fins. The male followed a short while later. I cannot at this stage say whether this fish practices any kind of brood care or whether the eggs developed at all. However, this event would seem to indicate that it is possible to breed *Bunocephalus* spp. in captivity.

The general hardness in my tank was 12° GH. I fed the fish on Tetra-Min and other Tetra flaked foods.

Michael Sallmann

Bunocephalus knerii Photo. W. A. Tomey

THE AUCHENIPTERID CATFISHES

Until a few years ago, the South American catfish family Auchenipteridae was known to aquarists by only two species: The Zamora cat *(Auchenipterichthys thoracatus)* and the wood, or driftwood, cat (any of several species of *Parauchenipterus)*. The Zamora cat's appeal to hobbyists comes from its very graceful, sharklike swimming motion and most acceptable community tank demeanor. Wood cats, on the other hand, have little to attract any but the most avid catfish fancier. Dull of coloration and secretive in habit, this fish was a poor harbinger of the fascinating diversity of forms that has more recently become available to American aquarists.

Of the family's more than 75 known species, about a dozen are now available to hobbyists willing to scour the trade for new arrivals. Among them are the strikingly patterned jaguar cat, *Liosomadoras oncinus,* the diminutive *Trachelyichthys exilis,* and an elongate striped species with the nearly unprocounceable name *Trachelyopterichthys taeniatus* recently imported under the name "Mandubi cat".

An undescribed Auchenipterichthys species. Photo: AquaLife Magazine/Japan

The Zamora cat, Auchenipterichthys thoracatus. Photo: P.V. Loiselle

Generally, auchenipterids are nocturnal, venturing out of hiding only at dark. With a bit of luck, one can sometimes coax one into view with food, the fish's tolerance to light lasting only as long as its hunger. As suddenly as it appears out of a crevice in the rockwork at the blink of an eye, it masterfully vanishes to a spot unknown.

The fleeting glances of a feeding auchenipterid offer a brief, but enticing glimpse of their graceful mode of swimming. For a better view, one must enter the catfishes' world of darkness. The hobbyist's ticket to that world is red light. Whether it comes from a second aquarium hood with small red bulbs, a photographer's safe-light somewhere in the room, or even a flashlight covered with red cellophane, limiting the light to red is an effective compromise between the human need for light and the catfishes' aversion to it.

In the dark, their motion is transformed from frantic scurrying for food to slow steady cruising from end to end of the tank. Both the gracefil eel like undulations of *Trachelyopterichthys* and the curious wiggle of *Trachelyichthys* are often accompanied by outstretched barbels directed upward. The dyed-in-the-wool bottom dwellers, such as *Liosomadoras,* may still just sit on the bottom, but at least ther's a better chance that the'll be out in plain view!

As with almost every group of fish, some auchenipterids like to do things differently. Members of the genus *Auchenipterus* are active

79

The jaguar cat, Liasomadoras oncinus, most spectacularly colored of the currently available auchenipterid catfishes. Photo: Carl J. Ferraris, Jr.

swimmers, constantly moving throughout the tank any time of the day or night. They prefer, however, subdued light and don't do well in brightly illuminated community tanks. When schooling, *Auchenipterus* looks like a pale irridescent shark, *Pangasius sutchii*, at first glance, and has fooled several advanced aquarists. However, the four long barbels at the tip of the lower jaw quickly give away its true identity.

Most species are undemanding about living space. All, except *Auchenipterus*, seek shelter from light in rockwork, vrevices in wood, or dense rooted vegetation. Opaque plastic tubing offers satisfactory shelter, but take care to increase the diameter of the tubing periodically as the fish grows. This precaution thereby prevents fin-spine deformation from continual contact with the unyielding shelter. Water chemistry may be quite varied without stressing the fishes, though soft acid water is most similar to their natural environment. *Trachelyichthys* seems not to tolerate large water changes well. Smaller, more frequent changes are thus advised.

Feeding auchenipterids is no problem. Most established aquarium residents readily accept a wide variety of living and prepared foods, an none seem particularly eager to consume tank mates in communities. The "catfish" habit of

The marbled driftwood cat, a small undescribed Parauchenipterus species from the Rio Parana basin.

bottom feeding doesn't apply to all. Some species will quickly find their way to the surface at feeding time. The actively swimming *Auchenipterus* also accept surprisingly fine particulate food for fish their size. Many members of the family, however, are quite shy. Given their preference for darkness, a late feeding best insures that these fish get their share of food.

Sexing auchenipterids is comparatively easy, by catfish standards. In adult males, the first few rays of the anal fin thickened and elongated, giving its margin a notched appearance in long-finned species. The maxillary barbels of some species are also modified, becoming thickened and elongated in mature males. A few species go even one tep further. The male's dorsal spine becomes long and spiny, and the fish itself may develop a humpedback appearance.

Little is known about auchenipterid courtship and repreoduction, but what has been discovered sets the family apart from other catfishes. In many, and perhaps all, species fertilization is internal, the sperm being directed into the females body by the thickened anal rays. Even more interesting, the females seem able to store sperm. They can thereby postpone depositing eggs until a later date. No one knows yet why this happens, or how to create the proper environment for egg deposition. However, the implicati-

The driftwood cat, one of the many Parauchenipterus species. Photo: P.V. Loiselle

An undescribed Auchenipterichthys native to the Peruvian Amazon.

The polka-dot cat, latia intermedia, a dwarf auchenipterid catfish.
Photo: AquaLife Magazine/Japan

The sinuous grace of Trachelyopterichthys taeniatus is typical of many members of the family Auchenipteridae. Photo: AquaLife Magazine/Japan

ons of this behavior for the fish breeder are two-fold. first, convincing the fish to copulate is only half the battle. Even a successful spawning embrace may not lead to immediate egg deposition. Providing conditions acceptable to the female may prove a challenge all its own.

The second implication is that it may be possible to "spawn" wild caught adult auchenipterid females at least once without first having to find a male! As these fishes are often brought in as "contaminants", and usually arrive in ones and twos, finding a breeding pair can be a difficult task. Even While searching for a male companion, an aquarist may be able to induce the female to deposit the first batch of eggs all alone. This has been successfully accomplished only with the help of hormone injections under laboratory conditions so far. However, it is likely that the efforts of dedicated aquarists eventually will produce the same results.

With the exception of some of the smaller armored catfishes, such as *Corydoras, Hoplosternum,* and *Rineloricaria,* there has been little success in breeding catfishes in aquaria to date. The recent introduction of several attractive species of Auchenipteridae into the hobby may expand this list and provide an opportunity to popularize these interesting, but little known fishes.

Dr. Carl J. Ferraris, Jr.

HOPLOSTERNUM CATFISHES

Some hobbyists call them ugly, some call them interesting and some even give them priority in their piscicultural interest. For whatever the reason, the catfish of the genus *Hoplosternum* have a place in the aquarium.

South America offers us a wide variety of catfish, from the very large shovelnose, *Pseudoplatystoma fasciatum,* to the dwarf *Corydoras* species. Somewhere in between fall most representatives of the family Callichthyidae or armored catfish, so called because of a series of overlapping bony plates which cover their flanks and in some species, the back of the head. The family Callichthyidae has been broken down into a number of genera, among them *Callichthys, Brochis, Dianema, Corydoras* and *Hoplosternum.* In this article, I deal with the latter, the catfish of the genus *Hoplosternum.*

Hoplosternum means amored breast. These catfish have an elongated cigar-shaped body, a broad, flattened head, and a very deep caudal peduncal. Their eyes are relatively small, but their upper jaw barbels can reach beyond the ventral fins.

For the size of their body they have a small rounded dorsal and an adipose fin supported by a spine. The bony protective covering these fish possess allows them to resist parasites. All are airbreathers that regularly "gulp" air at the surface.

Above and right: Hoplosternum littorale, Hoplosternum thoracatum, Hoplosternum sp. Photos: Delores Schehr

Hoplosternum are found from southern Panama throughout South America. They inhabit the enormous swamps associated with such rivers as the Amazon, Orinoco, Magdalena and Paraguay. These fishes have been known to science for over 150 years and are well established in the aquarium. The species available to hobbyists have been imported from Brazil, Paraguay, Columbia and Peru.

The genus *Hoplosternum* has three nominal species. *Hoplosternum thoracatum, H. littorale* and *H. pectorale* which may possibly be a junior synonym of *littorale*. In recent years, aquarists have also been able to enjoy a number of dwarf species. Their actual number remains to be determined by the scientific community. However, my own experience and that of several fellow hobbyists leads me

The popular porthole catfish, Dianema longibarbis.

to believe there are three separate and undescribed dwarf *Hoplosternum* species.

Hoplosternum thoracatum is so named because of its armored chest or thorax. The color of this species varies with the collecting locality but most resemble the fish in the accompanying photo. The caudal on this fish is squared off or has a straight edge. This fish averages between 15 and 20 cm (6" to 8") in the aquarium. *Hoplosternum littorale* is the largest species of the genus, reaching 20 to 22.5 cm (8" to 9"). It differs from *H. thoracatum* in having a rounded caudal fin. The last representatives of this genus are the fish referred to as the dwarf *Hoplosternum* species. As I have previously stated, this catch-all category may well comprise three separate species. The first dwarf hoplo cats I acquired were brown with few or no markings on their bodies. Their total length was 6.25 to 7.5 cm (2.5" to 3") which enabled them to be kept and spawned in a 22.7 liter (5 gallon) aquarium. The second dwarfs I acquired were approximately the same size as the previous fish. They differed noticably in color, however. This second fish was beige markged with little blotches to give a salt and pepper effect. The last dwarf *Hoplosternum* "species" is very similar to the second but the dark markings are smaller. The major differences between this fish and the previous two dwarf hoplo cats are behavioral, however. The third dwarf form defends its eggs much more aggressively than do other representatives of the genus and also appears to protect the mobile young in the bargain.

Hoplo cats are undemanding aquarium residents. A temperature range of 21° to 25°C (c. 70° to 80°F) suffices for day to day maintenance. They seem indifferent to water chemistry as long as extremes of pH and hardness are avided. They are more resistant to polluted water than many other aquarium fish, though it is no excuse for sloppy maintenance practices. Even the more robust species will not bother smaller tankmates. Because these are unaggressive catfishes, they should not be kept with such belligerent tankmates as the larger cichlids. Hoplo cats eat a wide variety of live and prepared foods. Pelletized foods, like TabiMin and Tetra-Tips are particularly appreciated. Newly introduced specimens are usually reluctant to take food from the surface. However, they soon overcome their shyness and compete effectively with their tankmates at feeding time.

When in good condition, *Hoplosternum* are not difficult to spawn.

Condition them by increasing the protein content of their diet. Frozen adult brine shrimp, tubifex worms, white worms, chopped earthworms, or a beef heart mixture are good examples of higher protein foods. Nor is sexing these fish difficult once they have reached maturity. Well-conditioned females get full in the abdomen, while the males are slimmer and larger overall. The first rays of the male's pectoral fins are also much thicker than those of the female. Furthermore, these thickened rays are reddish-orange in color. The females pectoral fins, in contrast are entirely clear. Spawning tank need be no larger than 90 liters (20 gallons). It should be filled half way up with water c. 23°C (76°F). In the wild, hoplo cats encounter a wide range of temperatures from as low as 15°C (50°F) up to 27°C (90°F), so temperature is not too critical. Since these fish

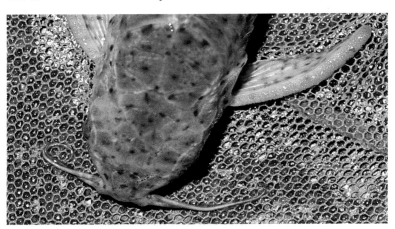

Note the enlarged, red pectoral fin spines of this secually active male H. thoracatum. Photo: Delores Schehr

A spawning pair of H. littorale under the male's massive bubble nest.

Photo: Delores Schehr

are bubble nest builders at spaw-ning time you must give them something to build their nest under. I have used receptacles ranging from coffee can lids of varying colors to a large 20 cm (8") plastic bowl turned upside down in the water. Of course, I was careful to remove the air from under the bowl so it would float properly! I found that breeding fish, given a choice of spawning sites, consistently selcect a colored lid under which to con-struct their "nest".

Although gravel wasn't used in the breeding aquaria, I always put in several 20 to 40 cm (8" to 12") long pieces of 7.5 and 10 cm (3" and 4") diameter PVC pipe. This what gives the female sufficient hiding places to be able to avoid contact with an overly aggressive male when necessary. A box filter filled with carbon and filter floss comple-tes the tank's furnishings. Obvious-ly, it must be adjusted to filter very slowly to keep from disturbing the male's nesting efforts. The pair should be kept separate while being conditioned. Then when the male and female are reunited he will show immediate interest by chasing her about. The male then begins depositing large bubbles under the lid. He goes to the surface to take in air, then releases saliva-coated bub-bles from his mouth under the lid. He continually attempts to persuade the female to show an interest in his nest. She eventually checks it out. If everything seems alright, he will then assume a vertical position under the nest.

The females appears to draw sperm from him into her mouth. She then swims to the tank bottom. When

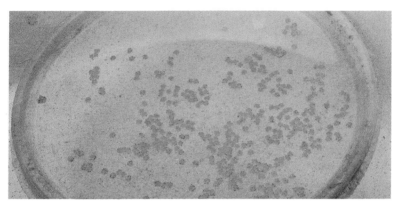

Fertile eggs of the dwarf hoplo cat. Photo: Delores Schehr

she comes back, she has eggs between her ventral fins. She then rises to the nest and from an upside down position places the eggs and sperm into the nest. Spawning can take serveral hours to complete. Clutches of about 100 eggs are the norm for the dwarf hoplo cats. The larger species can spawn up to 300 eggs.

As a rule, properly conditioned pairs spawn freely. Reluctant pairs will often respond to a major water change. Replacing half to three quarters of the breeding tank's volume with cooler water mimics the onset of the seasonal rains that trigger spawning in nature. It also can be helpful to add some floating plants to the breeding tank. *Hoplosternum littorale* in particular seems to appreciate the availability of plant malter to incorporate into its nest.

After spawning is completed, the male drives the female away. He then assumes a position under the nest to stand gaurd over his clutch of eggs. Hatching typically takes about four days. With the exception of the third dwarf hoplo cat I mentioned earlier, these catfish do not seem to look after their free-swimming fry. It is therefore a good idea to remove the male from the breeding tank once hatching has begun. It is also possible to hatch the eggs without the male by gently scooping out the lid and its associated nest and transferring it to a freshly set-up nursery tank.

The fry become free-swimming a couple of days after hatching. I start them off with microworms, then change to newly hatched brine shrimp nauplii in a few days time. The fry are very hardy. I move them into large 180 liter (40 gallon) rearing tanks as soon as possible to avoid the harmful effects of crowding. Under these conditions, their growth is rapid. All of the species I have bred will reach lengths of c. 3.0 to 3.5 cm (1 ¼" to 1 ½") within

6 to 8 weeks of spawning. Despite their rapid early growth, hoplo cats are relatively slow to mature. The dwarf species are old enough to spawn at eight months to a year old. *Hoplosternum thoracatum* and *H. littorale* take even longer, first breeding 18 months to two years postspawning.

Catfish are no longer solely relegated to their inferior position of "scavengers" they have held for so many years. Nowadays, many aquarists reserve their aquaria for their catfish collections! Because they are hardy and easily bred, the hoplo cats are an excellent choice for the beginning catfish enthusiast. Given due consideration to the space requirements of the larger *Hoplosternum* species, he can look forward to many years of pleasure from his armored pets.

Delores Schehr

◀ *Page 90/91: Corydoras panda. Photo: B. Kahl*

The attractively colored flagtail porhole cat, Dianema urostriata, has yet to be bred in captivity. Photo: P. V. Loiselle

THE ARMORED CATFISH OF THE GENUS CORYDORAS

The order of catfish, Siluriformes, consists of thirty-one or more different families, distinguished by a variety of features. There are gigantic species, such as the 8' (2.5 m) long *Pangasianodon* from the Mekong River, and tiny catfish no longer than an inch or so. There are heavily armored knights such as the *Plecostomus* species and the almost jelly-like, ⅘" (19 mm) long dwarf *Malacoglanis gelatinus,* which lives under waterfalls in Colombia. However, only a few species are suitable for the aquarium.

The family Callichthyidae includes the large genus *Corydoras,* the armored catfish, which are all ideal aquarium fish. At present over 100 species are known and new ones are always being discovered in the large river systems of South America. They are found from the La Plata Basin in the South to Venezuela in the north. Some are also found on Trinidad. Since the climatic range of their habitats spans 59 to 86°F (15 to 30°C), one should always ask the exact origin of such fish when purchasing them. The temperatures at which they are to be kept will depend to a large extent on this fact. Although the armored catfish are hardy and adaptable they are known to survive temperatures of almost 104°F (40°C) - keeping them constantly at any abnormally high temperatures

Corydoras barbatus. Photo: Rosario LaCorte

Above: Brochis splendens, a robust relative of the popular genus Corydoras with a similar reproductive pattern. Photo: B. Kahl

will soon exhaust them. In the wild they prefer shallow water over a mud or sand bottom, along the edges of small streams and larger rivers. They are frequently found in small, clear, slowly flowing streams, briskly dashing around in small shoals, constantly searching for food, and stirring up the bottom as they do so. They prefer to be close to thick plnat growths containing a lot of hiding places, and are often found hiding among the plants. They can be found even in areas where there is little water. Intestinal respiration enables them to breathe atmospheric air and even to remain on land for a limited period of time, using their pec-

The normal (above) and the albino (bottom) color form of the salt and pepper catfish, Corydoras paleatus.

Corydoras rabauti.

Corydoras nattereri.

The bronze catfish, Corydoras aeneus.

Corydoras shultzei.

Above: C. haraldshultzi.   *Below: C. melanistius*

toral fin rays as a means of locomotion. Ideally, the water in the aquarium should be no deeper than 16" (40 cm). It should be remembered that even under normal circumstances, when the water contains sufficient oxygen, they still gulp in atmospheric air at the surface.

A good growth of plants, covering the surface in some places, and all kinds of hiding places are advisable, although the surface of the water should not be completely covered with a thick mat of floating plants. A catfish tank also should have a good filter, otherwise their habit of rooting and burrowing in the gravel will result in a constantly cloudy tank. The armored catfish seem to possess a special kind of inquisitiveness as they roll their eyes attentively. They quickly get used to their keeper, but they always retain a certain sensitivity with regard to

C. arcuatus.

C. metae.

C. reticulatus.

C. trilineatus. Photo: P.V. Loiselle

vibrations. Mine, for example, take flight immediately when our dog runs across the room. A large collection of various armored catfish, kept by themselves in a long tank of 26 gal (100 l) or more, can be very interesting.

If you would like to breed them it is particularly necessary to have a large number of breeding fish. Experienced breeders recommend a ratio of twice as many males as females. At the beginning of the courtship the females swim restlessly around the tank or go up and down the glass sides, while the males swim around them tirelessly. The females also clean off spots on the sides of the aquarium. finally a male succeeds in pressing the barbels of the female to his body with one of his pectoral fins. The female then drops a small number of eggs, about 3 to 5, which are caught by her ventral fins formed into a pouch. the male has previously released sperm into the water. The

Corydoras axelrodi.

female, once released by the male, sticks the eggs to one of the cleaned spots or quickly cleans a new one for this purpose. This procedure is repeated until the female's supply of eggs is exhausted. As this varies according to the species, it can range anywhere between 30 to 1000 eggs. The size and age of the female are also of importance but the females should not be too fat. If the fish are hungry, which they almost always are, the eggs are eaten immediately. So it is advisable to put some food into the tank during spawning.   *ADI Staff*

C. elegans. Photo: P.V. Loiselle

PYGMY CORYDORAS, CORYDORAS PYGMAEUS

Until now this attractive little armored catfish has been considered as a subspecies of *Corydoras hastatus* and known as *Corydoras hastatus australe*.

According to Knaack, however, it is a distinct species which differs markedly from *C. hastatus*. This does not mean to say they are not closely related. Its body form and behaviour are somewhat different from that of the other species and for this reason many authors call it *Microcorydoras*.

The fish are small and have a very dainty appearance. There are 22 overlapping bony plates positioned above and 20 below, as in *C. hastatus* and it has three pairs of barbels at its mouth. the maximum length seems to be 2.5 cm. The body is brownish and grey coloured, sometimes with a beige tint. There is an intense black longitudinal stripe, extending from the mouth along the middle of the body before ending in an oval or ellipse-shaped mark at the root of the tail. The belly is coloured a matt shade of white. There is a dot visible in both eyes and also at the upper edge of the gill covers and under certain light conditions this takes on a silvery sheen. It has an adipose fin. Usually the sexes can only be distinguished at spawning time when the female's much stouter appearance is noticeable. Generally, the male appears somewhat slimmer and has a rather more pointed dorsal fin. Also, the black longitudinal stripe looks rather duller in the female and the one on her stomach is occasionally incomplete. Its natural range is limited to a few areas in the Amazon region.

The pygmy corydoras, C. pygmaeus. Photo: B. Kahl

These *Corydoras* prefer clear water with lots of hideaways and dense vegetation, though they also need plenty of free swimming room. However, they do settle down well in small containers. They have a particular liking for carpets of algae and a dense coating of fine humus and decaying vegetation, for these offer both hiding places and additional sources of food. These fish probably feel more at home with a good surface aerating device than with other types of filtration equipment. After all, loke all species of *Corydoras,* they possess an accessory respiratory organ. This allows them to breathe oxygen by taking in a gulp of air with the mouth and forcing it through the intestine. The oxygen is extracted by the hindgut. I have often ssen them dart up to the surface so quickly that I could scarcely follow them with my eyes and then they just glide gently back down to the bottom. They will take food from the open water but are also very fond of foraging about on the bed of the tank.

The best temperature to keep them at is around 20-24°C (68-75°F). There must be certain reservations as to whether they should be kept in community tanks because these little *Corydoras* are often regarded as items of food by some of the larger inhabitants of the aquarium and are hunted down as prey. This is parti-

Corydoras pygmaeus Photo: B. Kahl

cularly true of young fish up to 1.5 cm in length. Otherwise, they are very undemanding, dainty and gragarious creatures. Nor do they have any special requirements with regards to food and water conditions. However, in the breeding season they should be given some live food from time to time. Breeding them is a matter which requires some care. It is preferable to keep several males to one female. Optimum temperature at this time is between 24 and 26°C (75 to 78°F). They can be bred at temperatures around 20-22°C (60-71°F) but the yield will not be as high.

Well decorated tanks should be used because all attempts at persuading these corydoras to breed without proper decoration and a suitable bed have failed. The water must be quite fresh and crystal clear. When filling the tanks I added AquaSafe. Once they have been transferred to the breeding tank, it takes 4-5 days for the fish to settle down, at which point a little more fresh water can be added. Once the corydoras start to show signs of a readiness to spawn, one pair will split away from the rest. The male conducts his courtship while swimming around, positioning himself across the female's path, writhing and quivering. This pose lasts for about 3-4 seconds. When the female indicates that she is ready to mate, the male wraps himself around the female, by grasping the female's barbels between his pectoral fins and his body, before finally releasing his sperm. This also takes 3-4 seconds. After repeating this procedure a number of times, the two fish sink slowly to the bottom and remain lying there for about 8-10 seconds, motionless. One can assume that actual fertilisation takes place now, between the male sperms and the female egg, which is then released into the female's "egg pouch", formed by her ventral fins. The egg can be clearly seen emerging from the anal aperture. Afterwards the two fish set themselves in motion once more and the female starts to look for a suitable place to deposit the egg.

While she is doing so, she is usually attended by several other males intent on paying court to her once again, which means that she now has the twofold task of depositing the egg and warding off the attentions of the male suitors. Sometimes this can last for quite a while. Once she has found a suitable place for her egg - be it on the plants or on the aquarium glass - the spot is meticulously cleaned and the egg attached to it. Copulation then takes place again within 15-20 seconds. It is only after 3-4 eggs that the female takes a well-deserved break of about 1 minute, after which she again announces her willingness to mate with the male by swimming around excitedly. She demonstrates her "arousal" by swimming on the spot, waving her ventral fins around and occasional-

Corydoras hastatus, the dwarf corydoras. Photo: Dr. Foersch

ly quivering her tail. The spawning procedure, from courtship to spawning takes about one minute.

Courtship and the release of sperm by the male always takes place close to the bottom (3-5 cm above the bed) and under no circumstances any higher than this. A female which has previously been fed on a nutritious and varied diet will lay some 40-60 eggs, of which only about a third will have been effectively fertilised. The whole spawning process takes around two and half to three hours. Although these dwarf corydoras do not tend to cannibalise their own eggs, as a precautionary measure the parents should be removed from the tank after spawning, because they may occasionally eat an egg when foraging for food. If kept at temperatures of 24-26°C (75-78°F), the young larvae hatch after 4-6 days. For 2-3 days they live off their yolk sac before moving on to infusorians. In the early stages they grow very quickly. The head with eyes and three black dots running at regular intervals from the belly to the tail can be easily made out.

Otherwise they look pale and transparent. They have a small white mark on their breast. After two weeks they are already 10 mm long and can take freshly hatched *Artemia*.

They can be fully formed after 4 weeks but at temperatures around 20°C (68°F) they take almost twice as long to develop. Growth slows down after about two months and you are almost led to believe that the young *Corydoras* will not get any bigger at all. However, they subsequently make a giant "leap", though this will, of course, depend upon the diet they are given. The young fish are not as shy as their parents and like to swim about in the open water. They are sexually mature at 6-7 months, though the female does not yet have her egg pouch.

A good friend of mine also breeds these delightful little creatures and has also had very successful results. He started out with four of them and within 6 months had 120, with which he was able to continue to breed.

This was in the period between October and April. But it is not just the winter months that are suitable for breeding *Corydoras,* for we breed them in July and August, too. Granted, the yield of young fish was not as high as in winter.

I was quite astounded by an answer I received from West Aquarium in reply to a question I put to them about the development of the pygmy corydoras.

They told me that this species had not yet been bred by them and this remained one of their objectives for the future. I would have thought that this would not have posed too many problems for West Aquarium!

Silvan Jockel

THE DORADIDAE:
BEST KEPT SECRET IN CATFISHES

After *Corydoras,* "plecostomus" or suckermouth cats *(Hypostomus* or *Ancistrus)* and, possibly, the upsidedown *Synodontis,* the catfishes best known and most widely kept by aquarium hobbyists are the talking or thorny catfishes of the South American family Dorodidae. While some species in this family such as *Lithodoras dorsalis* or *Pseudodoras niger,* may never be home aquarium fishes because of their great bulk, most are of a size suitable for home aquaria. The well-known talking catfish, *Amblydoras hancocki* and the striped Raphael catfish *Platydoras costatus*

have always made excellent additions to community aquaria due to their unusual appearance, undemanding nature, and good community manners.

The same could probably be said for most of the more than one hundred species in this family, if only they were more readily available in the hobby. But, unfortunately, less than a dozen species ever seem to make it out of South America. Many of these are so infrequently imported that they are unavailable to most aquarists.

The common names usually used for the family Doradidae, thorny

The talking catfish, Amblydoras hancocki.

The mottled doras, Doras eigenmanni. Photo: P.V. Loiselle

cats and talking cats, refer to two of the more noteworthy features of the group.

Spines or "thorns" in one or more rows on the lateral surfaces of the body are the single feature that distinguishes members of the family from all other catfish groups. These spines are found at the center or along the posterior margin of a single series of bony plates, or scutes, which usually extend the whole length of the body and, in some species, cover the entire side of the fish. When combined with the omnipresent dorsal and pectoral fin spines, these scute spines present a defensive armament second to none. "Talking" refers to the racket made by most, if not all, species which have been netted or otherwise donfined. This noise is generated by rasping the base of their pectoral spines against their shoulder bones. This scraping action has earned the fishes the reputation of being among the loudest noisemakers of aquarium-kept fishes.

Doradids can be subdivided into two main gropus, differing from each other not only in general appearance, but in behavior as well. The first includes the most commonly seen members of the family, often known as the Raphael cats. All have broad, flat depressed heads, stout pectoral spines with large serrations and, usually, unbranched thread-like barbels. These fishes are generally very secretive, requiring rockwork

Above: Platydoras costatus, the stripped Raphael cat. Photo: P.V. Loiselle
Below: The spotted Raphael cat, Agamyxis pectinifrons. Photo: P.V. Loiselle

hiding places which they leave only for food and an occasional noturnal foray over the tank bottom. Besides the two species mentioned above, the round-tailed striped Raphael *Acanthodoras spinosissimus,* and the spotted Raphael *Agamyxis albomaculatus,* make it to the U.S. hobbyist market. Even more rarely, the large, but attractive, snail-eating

A Hildadoras species, one of the "rough" doradids.
Photo: AquaLife Magazine/Japan

Megalodoras inwini has been imported. The second group of doradids consists of species having more slender bodies, with much less depressed and often laterally compressed heads.

The pectoral spines are usually much less robust and their serrations finer. Their mouths are ventrally places, often with a tubular opening directed towards the substrate. The jaw teeth in these fishes are few and feeble, and sometimes absent entirely.

This contrasts with the toothy jaws of the Raphaels. The mouth is ringed with three pairs of barbels. These often appear feathery due to their numerous pinnately arranged small banches. These species are known in the trade as mouse cats,

Sierra cats, or zipper cats. Although also nocturnal, these fishes are more likely to be seen in community aquaria than are Raphaels. Instead of hiding in rockwork or its equivalent, they spend the light hours in the shadowy reaches at the back of the tank.

At night, they can be seen diligently searching the substrate for food with their taste bud laden barbels. When appropriately stimulated, the mouth protrudes downward and vaccuums up everything.

Once inside the mouth, sand, debris and other unwanted material are sorted from the food and ejected through either the mouth or gill openings.

Although no mouse cats come into the trade routinely, several species

Above: A giant doradid catfish, Megaladoras cf. irwinei.
Below: An unidentified Doras species. Photos: AquaLife Magazine/Japan

have been imported recently into the New York area from Guyana and the upper Amazon.

These include *Hemidoras microstomus* and the elongate *Leptodoras linelli*. One of the most interesting doradids to be imported in recent times, *Orinocodoras eigenmanni,* the long-nosed striped Raphael also belongs in this group.

Unlike its near look-alike, *Platydoras,* the attractive *Orinocodoras*

Above: A juvenile of one of the several unidentified Opsodoras species sold under the trade names of mouse, zipper or tershuki cat. Photo: P.V. Loiselle

Below: A smooth doradid catfish of the genus Hassar.
                    Photo: AquaLife Magazine/Japan

Opsodoras sp., close-up of head. Note the branched mandibular barbels, reminiscent of thos of the African Synodontis species. Photo: P.V. Loiselle

is much more active during the day. A fourth species, *Pseudodoras niger,* is often seen in public aquariums and occasionally can be found, as juveniles, under the name Dolphin Cat.

Captive maintenance of doradids is not difficult. They tolerate a wide variety of water conditions and temperature regimes. In fact, doradids have, all too often, been introduced into a community tank where their reclusive behavior causes them to be forgotten, and assumed dead. They are then typically rediscovered, fatter and much larger, at some later date.

Feeding doradids poses no special problems either. When offered live food such as Tubifex worms or even frozen bloodworms, many individuals can be enticed out of hiding, even in well-lit tank. If live foods are unavailable, pelletized sinking foods such as Tetra's Tabi-Min are readily accepted. A brief note about handling doradids is in order here.

Removing a specimen from a tank can be traumatic - for its keeper, not for fish - if not done with care and forethought. A dipnet rarely survives an encounter with one of these "rhorny" cats, with spines virtually everywhere on the body armed. The catfish becomes so thoroughly emeshed that often, the only way to extricate it is to cut the net into pieces!

As long as the fish remains moist through the operation, this seems to cause little stress to the animal. Several alternatives to this situation are available. The fish can be coaxed into a plastic cup or strainer. Alternatively it can be transferred along with its PVC shelter to its new home. However, I prefer to

The mandibular barbels of L. linelli are almost feathery in appearance.
Photo: AquaLife Magazine/Japan

capture these fish by hand. Covering the head and eyes with one hand usually calms the fish down and facilitates the transfer. Caution is required here, though. The pectoral spines will clamp down on anything between them and the fish's body, holding an errant finger as a painful hostage until released by its resubmerged captor.

Finally, along with "talking" and an occasional pinched finger, handling doradids results in yet another suprise for the uninitiated aquarist: the excretion of a milky white fluid from the region of the pectoral fin. The fluid's composition and its effect on other fishes is not yet known.

However, when disturbed, a large fish, or several smaller ones, can cloud a tank sufficiently to challenge the best filtration system. While the exudate seems not to be toxic to other fishes, it is best to avoid exposing them to it until more is known about the composition and effects of this fluid. Virtually nothing is known about reproduction in doradids. Sexual dimorphism is unknown, while to the best of my knowledge, none has been bred under aquarium conditions.

While this is undoubtedly due in part due to the rarity of the fishes in the hobby, it may also be function of the way in which they are usually maintained.

Widely perceived and kept as "cleaner" cats, they are often found as single individuals in a large com-

Leptodoras linelli, a very slender-bodied doradid species.
Photo: AquaLife Magazine/Japan

munity tank. Such a situation is not at all conductive to breeding! We are just now beginning to get a glimpse of the interesting biological and behavioral attributes of doradid catfishes. As more species are kept and observed, rather than relegated to the unenviable role of tank cleaner, the number of "secrets" surrounding these poorly known fishes should diminish dramatically.

Dr. Carl J. Ferraris, Jr.

An overview of the family Loricariidae

The armored, sucker-mouthed catfishes (Family: Loricariidae) are an extremely diverse group of primarily South American origin. The family comprieses over 600 species allocated among 70 genera. Variety is a keynote of this group of catfishes. Loricariids range in size from the diminutive *Otocinclus* species to such giants as *Hypostomus, Pterogoplichthys* and *Isorhinoloricaria.* Some species are active during the day, others at dusk or dawn, while many species forage only at night. Representatives of this group can be found in swiftly-flowing rapids, small forest creeks, the main channels of large rivers, oxbow lakes and even swamps. It is thus hardly surprising that the family offers something for every aquarist, regardless of how much tank space at his disposal or his other fish-keeping interests.

Such variety notwithstanding, loricariids share several common features. Like all catfishes, they are scaleless. However, their bodies are covered by protective armor-like bony plates. The mouth always

Page 114/115 Acanthicus hystrix Photo: B. Kahl ▶

A rarely imported loricariid catfish, the polka-dot plecostomus Pseudorhinelepis pellegrini. Photo: Joseph Mancusi

opens downward and has the form of a sucking disk. The jaws are well equipped with multiple rows of teeth. All can control the amount of light entering their eyes by means of a contractile pupil. The iris of the eye is generally shaped like the Greek letter omega and most species have a adipose fin, but exceptions to both characterizations are known. All the species to date bred in captivity or sudied in the wild practice exclusively male care of their large, adhesive eggs.

Most aquarists initially purchase an armored sucker-mouthed cat as a "worker fish" to keep their tank's glass walls and interior furnishings clean and free of algae. Subsequent purchases are usually based upon the subject's strange or attractive appearance. It is only with the passage of time that most hobbyists grow to appreciate these catfishes for their interesting behavior, whose complexity is sufficient to afford them a distinctive "personality" seldom encountered in other groups of aquarium fishes. A discerning eye is in order when purchasing loricariids. Badly torn or even abraded fins are not uncommon among newly imported specimens. Given the amazing regenerative powers of

The extraordinary nasal tentacles of the chocolate panque set it apart from the other Pterygoplichthys species to date imported. Photo: P.V. Loiselle

The mouth of the chocolate panaque. Such an array of large teeth is characteristic of most large loricariids. Photo: P.V. Loiselle

these catfish, they should not deter the purchase of an otherwise interesting subject. The same cannot be said for signs of extreme malnutrition. Most armored sucker-mouthed catfishes are deprived of food for several days prior to shipping. This allows them to purge their intestinal tracts before they are bagged, an absolutely essential precaution given the quantities of waste even a single specimen can produce over a period of several hours. Thus newly imported specimens usually appear to be on the thin side. However, individuals that are clearly hollow-bellied and whose eyes appear to have sunken into their sockets are victims of prolonged starvation. They should never be purchased, as their condition is terminal and cannot be corrected. Medium-sized to large loricariids are usually sold under the catch-all names "plecostomus" or "pleco",

Acanthius hystrix, the lyre-tailed polka-dot panaque.

117

Its elevates number of dorsal fin rays places this unidentified Peruvian species in the genus Pterygoplichplichthys. Photo: P. V. Loiselle

often prefaced with some descriptive word or phrase. Slender-bodied species are often offered for sale as "whip-tailed catfish". This practice does nothing to aid in correctly identifying these catfish. Such efforts are of more than academic interest, for the behavior of loricariids varies markedly between species. As will become evident, adding a large armored sucker-mouthed cat to an established community tank in ignorance of its behavior can have unpleasant consequences for all concerned.

Equally important, juvenile loricariids give little hint of their eventual adult size. Many species can exceed 60 cm (c. 2') in overall length. It is obviously preferable to have a clear understanding of what one is taking on before rather than after adding such a robust newcomer to a collection of fishes! The prospective buyer of a "pleco" that looks somewhat different in appearance should make a point of asking at the time of purchase if the shop owner knows where the shipment containing the fish originated. Even if he should answer in the negative, he might be persuaded to contact his supplier with a request for such information. Knowing its country

The zucchini cat, Isorhinoloricaria festae, so named because of its preferred diet in captivity, is the largest loricariid to date exported. Photo: P.V. Loiselle

A junvenile of the boldly patterned royal panaque, Panaque nigrolineatus.
Photo: P.V. Loiselle

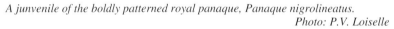

119

The cheek bristles of this male Rhineloricaria species are clearly evident.

of origin can greatly aid future efforts to identify such a "mystery fish". All male loricariids are markedly territorial, while such behavior can be expected from all individuals in many species. As a rule, conspecifics are the usual targets of such aggression. However, some species will not tolerate the close presence of other loricariids, and in a few cases, even the addition of other types of catfish to their tank provokes a violent reaction. The intensity of such intolerance is frequently unappreciated because the majority of catfish conflicts occur after the tank lights go out. Never assume that there will be no future problems merely because all appears peaceful when a new catfish of any sort is introduced to an aquarium with established loricariid residents! This assumption can prove costly. Few naked catfishes can long withstand the attacks of an irate loricariid and even other armored sucker-mouthed catfishes run a serious risk of injury or death under such circumstances.

Territoriality among the smaller species, e.g. *Otocinclus, Peckoltia* (clown plecos), *Ancistrus* (bristle nose plecos), *Farlowella* (twig catfishes), *Dasyloricaria, Rhineloricaria* or *Sturisomatichthys* (whiptail catfishes), is frequently overlooked, largely because its manifestations are not as overt as in the larger loricariids. However, even juveniles of such robust fgenera as *Panague* (blue-eyed and royal piecos), *Pterogoplichthys* (sailfin plecos) and *Pseudorhinolepis* can be violently intolerant of conspecifics. They will

chase and battle each other conti-
nuously, using their interopercular
and pectoral fin spines as dueling
weapons. Nor ought the capacity of
their powerful mouths, well equipped with teeth, to do damage be
underestimated.

Territorial disputes usually center
around availability of shelter. It is
thus sometimes possible to reduce
their incidence dramatically by
offering all the loricariids present
access to a suitable hiding place.
Rock caves, drilled-out pieces of
driftwood, clay flowerpots and sec-
tions of PVC pipe are all well
accepted. Fighting can also be
minimized by introducing all of an
aquarium's loricariid residents to
the tank simultaneously. A few

days of squabbling to establish a
stable pecking order will usually
ensue, but serious fighting is rare
under these circumstances. Bear in
mind that the territorial needs of
these catfish increase as they grow
larger, so an arrangement that satis-
fies the needs of several individuals
may prove inadequate with the passage of time.

Death by slow starvation is probably the greatest threat these catfish
face in captivity. Loricariids are
algae eaters in nature. Their hearty
appetites make it impossible to supply them with a supply of their
natural foods adequate for maintenance and growth under aquarium
conditions. Reports of "killer
plecos" that rasp the body mucus

*A strikingly marked dwarf loricariid of the genus Peckoltia, commonly known as
clown plecostomus. Photo: P.V. Loiselle*

121

As a close-up of the anterior half of its body clearly indicates, this Ecuadorian species can contend for the title of prickliest as well as largest loricariid catfish!
Photo: P.V. Loiselle

from the flanks of other fishes are a clear indication of such chronic malnutrition. Fortunately, there are plenty of acceptable substitute foods to choose from when planning a menu for these catfish. Newly purchased specimens should initially be offered sinking vegetable-based pellet foods supplemented with frozen bloodworms and well-washed Tubifex. Within short time, most individuals learn to take floating pellets such as Doro-Min and Doro-Green from the surface of the water. I have found that thinly sliced zucchini, parboiled to allow it to sink quickly to the bottom, is an invaluable addition to the diet of loricariid catfishes. It is rich in vitamin C, a necessity in the diet of all fishes. Furthermore, loricariid fry accept it readily and put on size rapidly when fed it on a regular basis. Many species will graze upon submerged wood so efficiently that their activity will literally "sand down" a piece of driftwood within a short period of time. Ther are even reports of large Panague rasöing their way through the epoxy layer of a wood and glass tank and thus causing a major leak, to the considerable chagrin of their owner! Apart from their insistance upon plenty of vegetable matter in their diet, armored sucker-mouthed catfishes are easily maintained. Like most lowland tropical fishes, they prosper when maintained at a tank temperature of 74°-78°F (c.

22°-24°C), with an increase of a few degrees for breeding. As a group, they are not picky about water chemistry. Loricariids will live and even breed over a wide range of pH and hardness values as long as extremes in either direction are avoided.

I have even kept *Hypostomus* and *Chaetrostoma* species for extended periods of time in brackish water (1 tsp marine salt/gallon) with no ill effects. However, all loricariids demand clean, well oxygenated water. This fact, no less than the copious quantities of solid wastes produced by the larger species, dictates the use of a powerful filter in their tanks. All of these catfish benefit from regular water changes. These are best carried out with the help of a Hydro-Clean, for their copious output of long fecal strings requires that the gravel in their tanks also be cleaned regularly.

Together with the respresentatives of the Family Callichthyidae, loricariids are among the very few catfishes that can regularly be induced to breed in captivity. This is at least partly due to the ease with which many species can be sexed. Many loricariids are stiningly sexually dimorphic. In many species, males are copiously endowed with fine bristles on their heads and pectoral fins. In *Farlowella,* these bristles occur on the snout and cheeks. In *Sturisoma* and *Sturisomatichthys,* they are present on the cheeks alone. Males of the true whiptailed cats of the genera *Loricaria, Rhineloricaria* and *Dasyloricaria* sport them on their heads, cheeks and

Page 124/125: Sturisoma migrirostrum Photo: G. Kilian ▶

Their dorsoventrally flattened bodies betray the butterfly plecostomus of the genus Lasiancistrus to be rapids-dwellers in nature. Photo: P.V. Loiselle

pectoral spines. In *Lasiancistrus, Isorhinoloricaria* and *Panaque,* they are restricted to the pectoral spines in these species, the longer the bristles and the greater their density, the greater the male's reproductive readiness. The branching, fleshy tentacles on the snout and head of male *Ancistrus* differentiate them clearly from females. Indeed, an observer unfamiliar with these fish would be forgiven for assuming the two sexes to belong to

A male royal whiptail catfish, Sturiso-matichthys sp., with his clutch of eggs. Photo: Joseph Mancusi

different genera! Even among such relatively isomorphic loricariids as *Hypostomus* and *Pterogoplichthys,* the thicker pectoral fin spines and pendant genital papillae of males makes it easy to tell the sexes apart. As long as they are well fed and provided with a suitable spawning site, isolated pairs of loricariids will usually spawn readily. The presence of a second male is an insurmountable distraction in most cases.

The two males spend all their time glaring at one another even in the presence of an obviously ripe female. The choice of spawning site varies considerably between species. *Otocinclus* place their eggs on broad-leafed plants, while *Farlowella* and *Sturisoma-tichthys* prefer a solid vertical surface, such as the tank walls. The true whiptail cats demand a tunnel or tube as a spawning site, while the larger loricariid genera such as *Ancistrus, Hypostomus* and *Pterogoplichthys* are cave spawners that often excavate their own spawning site in the bank of a stream in nature. In all instances, the male alone cleans the spawning site and provides all subsequent parental care, inclusive of chewing the fry free of their egg shells. There is no posthatching care, but if well fed, neither parent will molest their progeny. Loricariid fry hatch in five to seven days, depending upon water temperature.

Octocinclus vittatus Photo: P. V. Loiselle

They are immediately free-swimming and ready to feed. A mature sponge filter provides an important source of microscopic food for the newly emerged fry. *Ancistrus* and whiptail catfish fry can take blanched zucchini immediately. *Sturisomatichthys* fry require microworms and *Artemia* nauplii for their first three to five days of life, then can be offered blanched zucchini. After a week or so, prepared foods can be added to their diet. The fry are easily reared if due attention is paid to water cleanliness. Uneaten fresh vegetable foods such as blanched zucchini tend to foul the water in the rearing tanks rapidly. Hence they should be offered in small amounts. Regardless of the nature of their diet, loricariid fry grow best if half the water in their tank is changed every three to five days.

I have found that the loricarids I have bred mature very quickly under aquarium conditions. Whiptail cats begin breeding between five and six months of age, *Ancistrus* and *Sturisomatichthys* at just under a year old. There is no indication of such reproductive precocity in nature. Thus I suspect that the early onset of reproduction among these catfishes is largely a function of the greater availability of food in captivity. Whether this pattern holds true for the larger loricariid species remains to be determined.

Though several *Hypostomus* species and *Pterogoplichthys anisitsi* are regularly pondbred in Florida, aquarium spawnings of these armored giants are few and far between.

Ginny Eckstein

Eliminating algae from fresh-water aquariums using Hypostomus plecostomus

In spite of the best filtration (filter with mechanical pump, filter material of gravel and charcoal), best illumination (fluorescent lighting Vita lite, Gro-Lux, warm tone, switched on for 16 hours a day), only artificial light, a constant pH of 6.8-7.2, the sides of my aquariums, plants, stones and decorative roots were repeatedly covered with algae. Scrapers using blades or magnets are often just enough to keep the front glass clean but the glass may be easily scratched.

I searched for a better way and found the ideal solution in the addition of a single *H. plecostomus*. One medium-sized specimen (4-6 inches) completely cleaned my 44-gallon tank in one week. Not only the glass but also the stones, decorative roots and all the plants were

A large Hypostomus cf. plecostomus.

entirely free of algae and undamaged. As a result of this experience I have put these catfish, in various sizes, into all of my tanks. This hardworking species not only removes the algae but also all food remnants! They move around like tiny vaduum cleaners, gliding over any gravel with their mouths and sucking in all excess food.

Although the species does become quite large, it grows very slowly. They are peaceful, undemanding and, thanks to their good armoring, can be kept with aggressive species. My *H. plecostomus* are in tanks together with Malawi Cichlids and with Killifish. There have been no quarrels and no losses. Other fish which are referred to as algae-eaters (chinese algae eaters, *Otocinclus* species) have turned out to be useless. Although I always have about 20 specimens of these species they are nothing more than decoration. In tanks of predatory fish these species are often eaten, so that they cannot function for this purpose.

In conclusion, I can say that after more than two years of experience with these fish that *H. plecostomus* is probably the most useful freshwater fish.   *Horst Kleine*

BREEDING HYPOSTOMUS PUNCTATUS

I have been interested in the catfish *Hypostomus punctatus* for some time now, but I have been unable to find anything in the literature concerning their breeding requirements. In fact, most books say that they have not yet been bred in captivity.

In our holiday home we are fortunate to have three splendid 490 litre show tanks, and in one of these I keep various characins and a pair of *P. punctatus*. From the beginning this pair of catfish did not get on at all well with each other, with the male usually being the more aggressive. It is quite easy to distinguish between the sexes as the male is smaller and has larger barbels. Then one day in the autumn this anti-social behaviour changed, and all of a sudden they became the best of friends. They began to chase one another and play together - in short, the previous aggressive behaviour became a thing of the past!

I noticed that they then started to hang around one particular root, and this root had a thumb-sized hole in it due to decay. Each fish in turn started to disappear inside the hole, apparently cleaning it out. Then one morning (about 5 days after their change in behaviour) I noticed that they had spawned and deposited a clump of dark brown

The spotted plecostomus, Hypostomus punctatus.

eggs just inside the hole in the root. The male then took up guard duty over them and chased all and sundry away from the surrounding area - including the female! The male also ensured that the eggs were provided with a flow of fresh water by fanning them with his pectoral and caudal fins. After a few days the two white spots inside the egg changed into dark spots, reflecting changes in the developing fry inside.

About eight days after spawning the eggs suddenly disappeared from their location in the root, and it took me a few minutes to locate the male who was now hiding under the root, still fanning away. It was only when I shone a flashlight on the spot that I saw the fry clinging firmly to the underside of the roots, wriggling their little tails. It looked rather like a miniture version of bats hanging from a belfry! The male continued to guard them chasing all other fish, and even the snails, away from the area. However, this apparently efficient parental care could not have been completely effective as I noticed that the number of fry began to decline. I suspected that they were being eaten, but I never discovered by whom. Ten days after they had hatched, the fry were about 2 cm long and were feeding off the algae on the glass just like their parents. I fed the young catfish on TetraMin and TetraMin Tablets, and they were particularly fond of the latter.

Mönning

A BIG, BLUE-EYED, BLACK CATFISH

Recently a new, interesting type of catfish has been occasionally imported. The fish in question is *Panaque suttoni,* and, as such, related to the already well-known *Panaque nigrolineatus,* often traded under the name of royal catfish. The basic colour of the fish is a dark grey to almost black with a silvery sheen which varies in intensity with the light conditions. Out of this sombre background a pair of deep sky blue eyes gaze up at you and it is this surprising and impressive contrast which renders the fish such a charming and desirable subject.

The importer informed me that these catfish originate in fast-flowing mountain streams in Colombia, and the species therefore has a high oxygen requirement. This is apparent in the aquarium, because if the filtration and aeration are poor, the gill covers of the fish immediately start pumping heavily. They are practically omnivorous and will even take lettuce, boiled carrots as well as TetraMin and Tetra Conditioning Food. In addition, aquatic plants may be regarded as an item of food and consequently do not last very long! It is important for the aquarium to contain old roots or

A fine specimen of the blue-eyed plecostomus, Panaque suttoni.

pieces of bogwood. These catfish spend every night "gnawing" their way around this, so the wood always looks as if it has just been polished. It then appears that the gnawed-off wood filings represent an important dietary regulating agent for the catfish's digestive system. Fish of this size, for they grow up to 30 cm long, are clearly not going to be satisfied by merely grazing on hte natural growth of algae in the tank!

However, they do not grow at a tremendous rate. A young fish would have to be kept for a number of years before its length exceeded 20 cm. In large specimens very striking so-called "sideburns" are found, which vary in length from fish to fish. The whiskers of these sideburns grow out of a mobile, extensible part of the body, located below the eyes just in front of the base of the pectoral fin. I assume that the specimens with the long sideburns - in some cases up to more than 10 cm long - are males. In the females these growths seem to be only half this length, which would indicate that the specimen shown here is a female. Incidentally, these "whiskers" are very hard and the catfish use them to drive off rivals in squabbles and to defend their territories.

All in all, this is an interesting species, not least because there remains a great deal yet to be discovered about it. It makes a very interesting subject for study in large tanks where it may be kept together with other robust fish, such as cichlids.

Photo and text: Berthold Weber

PTERIGOPLICHTHYS GIBBICEPS - A SPECTACULAR DORICARIID CATFISH

Most catfish are notable for their interesting body forms, and rarely for their attractive colouration. *Pterigoplichthys gibbiceps* is an exeption, and as well as the interesting shape, it has a spectacular spotted pattern making it look something like an aquatic leopard! Another unusual characteristic of this species (of great importance to the aquarist) is that it is not only active during the night, but it can also be seen by day. The sucker mouth catfish from South America belong to the family Loricariidae, and comprises over a dozen different genera. The *Otocinclus* species are the midgets of the family, whilst *Hypostomus* species, thought to number more than 50, are amongst the giants, reaching a length of up to 30-50 cm. (These sizes are for wild

An adlut P. gibbiceps. The 6" flower pot in the background gives some notion of how large the sailfin plecostomus can really grow! Photo: Vince Edmundson

specimens, and are rarely reached in the aquarium.) The genus *Pterigoplichthys* with its best-known species *P. gibbiceps,* comes around the middle of the size scale, in the wild this catfish is said to reach 20 cm, but in the aquarium rarely exceeds 13-15 cm. *Pterigoplichthys* and *Hypostomus* are closely related genera, but a quick look at the dorsal fin will easily distinguish between them; *Hypostomus* species have one spiny and seven soft rays in their dorsal fin, whilst *Pterigo-* *plichthys* possesses one spiny ray and 10 to 13 soft rays making the dorsal fin appear larger.

A few specimens of *P. gibbiceps* have recently been imported and made available to aquarists, their size usually around 8-12 cm. As for all members of the Loricariidae, the water for *P. gibbiceps* should be well oxygenated and not too warm, as in their natural environment they live in strongly flowing, well aerated waters that are usually a few degrees cooler than their surroun-

Page 136/137: Hypancistrus zebra Photo: B. Kahl ▶

A strikingly marked juvenile Pterigoplichthys gibbiceps.

dings. As wide a variety of food as possible should be provided, and various live, flaked, and other foods are accepted; algae and TetraMin Tablets are a special treat.

Aquarists interested in keeping this species would be well advised to keep several individuals together as it is only then that their interesting territorial behaviour can be observed. Their disagreements over territories are usually over a better hiding place, and often involve firmly grasping the opponent with one's sucking mouth or attacking him with flailing fins! Fortunately injuries occur only rarely, and when they do it is usually only minor damage to the fins or skin which heals within a few days.

Keeping several together also gives the aquarist the chance of finding out their breeding requirements, and the fact that more and more members of the Loricariidae are being bred in captivity should offer encouragement, as well as providing appropriate hints. For example, it would appear that a drop rather than a rise in temperature is important for breeding, and it is likely that some kind of cavity may be necessary for spawning and rearing the brood. Caring for the fry may be another problem altogether, but again experience with other members of the family may help.

Keeping several *Pterygoplichthys gibbiceps* will in fact be rather expensive as individuals can cost more than tank-bred discus, but they do offer the aquarist a great deal in return. It is likely that this species will be seen more frequently in the future, and I am sure that eventually their requirements for successful breeding will be found.

Herbert Winkelmann

BREEDING ANCISTRUS DOLICHOPTERUS, THE BUSHY-MOUTHED CATFISH

As most interested aquarists will testify, the market is not exactly flooded with catfish. Most of those that are offered for sale are the small armored catfish, and only rarely are the more interesting species seen. One of the rarer species occasionally offered for sale is the bushy-mouthed catfish *Ancistrus dolichopterus*. Most keen aquarists will tend to buy on impulse when they find one on account of its extremely bizarre appearance. That is not to say that they are likely to regret their purchase for one moment!

A. dolichopterus grows to a length of 13 cm and should therefore only be kept in the larger aquarium. This species is a bottom dwelling fish and possesses a sucker-mouth which enables it to remain firmly against the substrate in even the strongest current. This behaviour, coupled with its dark brown colouration, often makes this species rather difficult to see in the aquarium. I purchased my two bushy-mouthed catfish from different pet shops, and much to my great delight, they turned out to be a pair. It is fairly easy to distinguish bet-

The large eggs of the bristle-nose plecostomus, shown slightly larger than life size, measure c. 2.0 mm across.

ween the sexes as the male possesses a growth of long thick "bristles" around the snout and on the head, whilst those of the female are thin and short.

I introduced my two new catfish into a thickly planted 130 litre tank, decorated with a number of sone terraces and roots, and already housing some armored catfish and a few characins. My initial hopes of getting this pair to breed rapidly disappeared as they appeared to take absolutely no notice of each other.

Fortunately this state of affairs changed when they had grown to a length of 9 cm, with the male starting to chase the female all over the tank. His intentions were quite cle-

View from above of the head of a male bristle-nose plecostomus, Ancistrus dolich-opterus.

Not all male Ancistrus develop the bizarre cephalic tassle of this specimen!
Photo: P.V. Loiselle

ar, but the female wanted nothing to do with him and avoided all his advances.

The time had now arrived for me to "join forces" with the male, so I lowered the pH and raised the temperature of the water slightly in the hope that this might bring the female into spawning condition. Success was not long in coming, and very soon eggs could clearly be seen shining through the female's belly. In the meantime the male had dug out a hole under the stone terraces by pushing aside the gravel with his large tail fin.

Three days later I discovered about 50-60 yellowish eggs in a packet sticking to the roof of the hollow spawning cavity. The male was hovering over the eggs like a worried hen, fanning water over them with his pectoral fins, he had alrea-dy partially closed the entrance to the cavity with gravel swept up using his tail.

I left the eggs with the male for several days and then on the fifth day I removed the terrace stones with the eggs still attached and put them into a small separate tank containing the same water; the male immediately lost all his paternal drive.

The next day about 30 fry hatched, but the rest of the eggs appeared to be unfertilised. The young were about 10 mm long, and already showed the typical brown colouration. At first I fed them on chopped scalded spinach and nettles, and later went over to Cyclops. Feeding the young turned out to be extremely difficult and despite all my efforts, only half the fry survived the first two critical weeks.

Both the fleshy cephalic tentacles and the grey preopercular spines mark this unidentified Ancistrus species a male.

Since those early days I have spawned the bushy mouthed catfish several times, and experience has shown that it is better to leave the eggs and the fry with the parents. Their chances of survival are far greater as long as there is an adequate supply of algae in the tank to feed them.

(Footnote: aquarium conditions - temperature 25°C; pH 6.3; hardness 15°dH. The tank was only weakly illuminated.)

Mathias Steinwachs

The male Ancistrus guards his spawning site. Several of his young can be observed on the face of the rock.

To learn more about catfishes and loaches...

Readers with a serious interest in learning more about these two groups of aquarium residents should consider joining the following specialty groups:

American Catfish and Loach Association
Contact: Mr. Lee Finley
151 North Road, Pascoag, RI 02859
Publication: Catalyst, 6 issues/yr.

Catfish Association of Great Britain
Contact: Mr. Mike Sanford
5 Sparrows Meade, Redhill, Surrey
United Kingdom RHI 2 ET
Publication: Catfish Association of Great Britain Magazine 4 issues/yr.

About the authors

Dr Paul V. Loiselle is an accomplished aquarist of over twenty years experience. The international published author of numerous articles on the care and breeding of aquarium fishes, he is a Contributing Editor for Freshwater and Marine Aquarium. Dr Loiselle has his Master's degree from Occidental College in Los Angeles, and took his doctorate at the University of California at Berkley. His professional background includes five years as a Peace Corps fisheries biologist in West Africa, where he carried out faunal and environmental impact surveys in Togo nad Ghana.

During the course of this career, Dr Loiselle ahs had the opportunity to observe the behavior of cichlids in Lakes Victoria and Tanganyika, in Mexico and in Central America. A founding member and Fellow of the American Cichlide Association, he currently serves th C.A. as Technical Editor of its journal, Buntbarsche Bulletin, and as Chairman of the Special Publications Commitee.

Dr. David Pool has been keeping fish for over 20 years and is well known for his radio interviews, TV appearances, lectures and magazine articles on the subject. After obtaining an Honours Degree in Zoology he was awarded a PhD for his studies on the diseases of koi. He subsequently lectured at Liverpool University and Liverpool Polytechnic in Animal Parasitology and Fisheries Biology. In 1985 Dr Pool became a consultant to Tetra and headed the Information Centre which provides advice to thousands of fishkeepers every year.